Y0-CCR-257

Why Kids Jump over the Moon

or
How to get along with children

by
Pearl Cassel

Guidance Centre

10 Alcorn Avenue, Toronto, Ontario M4V 2Z8

First Revised Edition 1985

Canadian Cataloguing in Publication Data

Cassel, Pearl, 1931-
    Why Kids Jump over the Moon, or, How to get along with children

ISBN 0-7713-0202-9

1. Teacher-student relationships.   2. Classroom management.
3. Parent and child.   4. Youth.
I. University of Toronto. Faculty of Education. Guidance Centre.   II. Title.
III. Title: How to get along with children.

LB1117.C37 1985   371.1'02   C85-098603-6

© *The Governing Council of the University of Toronto*

Acknowledgments

I wish to thank the following people for their support as I developed the various concepts in this book.

Firstly my appreciation goes to Edith Dewey because, as my study group leader in 1968, she introduced me to Adlerian psychology and to Dr. Rudolf Dreikurs.

To Jack Wallace, Co-ordinator of Guidance, Scarborough Board of Education, Ontario, for his caring and co-operation.

To Ruth Gaal, who accompanied me and encouraged me on many public speaking engagements and also recorded my class discussions for two years.

To Helen Singleton, a member of my first parent study group, who gave me so much help in my quest for understanding.

To my husband Sid Cassel for his devoted support and editing advice. And finally, to my son Paul for his loving patience.

P.G.C.

Foreword

Teachers, and parents are confused about training children. This book will help the reader to understand what goes on in the mind of a child. It will help a teacher to understand and correct misbehaviour of students and help parents to learn to live harmoniously with their children.

This is a collection of presentations given to thousands of teachers and parents throughout North America.

Pearl Cassel
May 1980

Contents

Introduction—Why Did Our Kids Jump over the Moon?

Chapter
1 Life-style Analysis 7
2 Birth Order and Personality 13
3 Typologies of Birth Order 16
4 Typologies of Life-Style 23
5 The Human Touch 35
6 Child Training 40
7 Discipline in the Classroom 47
8 Understanding Structure in a Primary Classroom 63
9 Parent Education—When and by Whom? 72
10 Understanding the Four Goals 77
11 Growth of the Self-concept in Youth 93
12 Understanding Teenagers 103
13 Communicating With Your Teenager 110
14 Awareness Especially for Counsellors 116

Charts
1 Suggested template for sibling ratings 33, 134
2 Decision-making 34, 135
3 A person needs encouragement 66
4 Class discussion guide 71
5 Identifying the four goals of misbehaviour 91
6 How to correct children's misbehaviour 92

7 Personality priorities 101
7a Negative and positive uses of the life-style 101
8 Intrapsychic cycle of discouragement 102
9 How to recognize and correct teenage misbehaviour . 109

Appendix
1 How to Analyse Your Own Life-Style 131
2 Dreikurisms 136

Introduction

Why Did Our Kids Jump over the Moon?

They believed that it would look better from the other side.

●

They assumed that something special was over there for them.

●

They went to paint the sun and color the rainbow.

●

Normal was not enough for them.

●

They aspired to brighter colors, greater passions, clearer insights and instant ecstacy.

●

They wanted to escape from their parents' hypocricies.

●

The sky was not the limit. Everything was possible, desirable, and also available.

●

It is a long and difficult struggle through the maze from childhood to responsible adulthood. It seems easier to want to jump up high—even over the moon. To keep one's feet on the ground offers little in thrills or excitement, and no satisfaction to youthful impulsiveness.

Impulsivity is the excitement and enemy of youth. It can drive them toward ambition but can also present them with the stumbling block that denies their arrival. Wise adults are guardians, because impulsivity ignores consequences. Kids live with parents but a short while before they fly from the nest. As parents, we love, nurture and guide our young. They respond to our love and give us love in return, and we are encouraged to pursue the enormous task of child training. We dutifully sacrifice and put forth tremendous efforts in hopes that our kids will eventually live happy and productive adult lives. But we have no guarantees that they will fit their lives into the pattern that we have created for them.

Our society is now a democratic one, based on the pursuit of happiness. Previous to modern times, however, the autocratic society that existed for thousands of years used *fear* and *hope* as motivators for thinking about the future as well as an effective social behaviour control. These two notions, supported by both state and church, successfully pacified people and held back their struggles for individual freedom. The hope for a better life after death modified personal goals. The fear of the wrath of God or the protectors of the state discouraged antisocial behaviour. For youth today, these methods of control are meaningless. They have discovered that lawyers can prove that a guilty man is innocent, politicians don't keep their promises and established religion is to be ridiculed.

So existentialism became a philosophy of life for many of the youth who rejected traditional values.

Existentialism

This controversial philosophy became very popular in France and Germany after World War II, but had its origins in the nineteenth century. Today many of our adolescents have accepted this viewpoint for life functioning.

The basic underpinnings for existential theory were written by Soren Kierkegaard (regarded as a crank and a nuisance in his home town of Copenhagen), during the 19th century. He raised questions such as—What is the point of man's life? What sense can he make out of human existence? What is the purpose of human events? Is there a method to all this madness?

He stated that human life is anguished and absurd, harrowing and meaningless. The solution to human problems lies in somehow being able to find a link between man's history and some sort of eternal knowledge. In today's society of fragmented families, youth asks such questions of their own lives, because they lack or have rejected traditional religious philosophies and rituals.

An attempt to find the missing link was made during the fifties by Aldous Huxley, and then in the sixties by Timothy Leary (and thousands of followers) as they experimented with peyote and L.S.D. in order to find fast answers through a stimulated awareness. In an hallucinogenic state, they believed, they approached the essence, clarity, and ecstasy of life.

Present existential humanist writers like Rollo May *(Love and Will)* and Viktor Frankl *(Man's Search for Meaning)* believe it is possible for man to find himself without the use of drugs. Frankl even found meaning through suffering in the concentration camps with the loving memories of his wife. Rollo May shows how we can, through the many forms of love, attain a deeper consciousness that will help us to rediscover human meaning and values amid the vast emptiness of our depersonalized technology. We can find a *natural* high by contributing to others. He states that there are four kinds of love in our Western tradition (and uses classical Greek terms to define them):

Libido—sexual love

Eros—the drive of love to create or aspire toward a higher relationship

Philia—brotherly love and friendship

Agape—love devoted to the welfare of others.

Alfred Adler devoted much of his thinking to Agape. He called it *gemeinschaftsgefuhl*, or social interest. He believed that a sense of meaning to existence comes from feeling useful, helping others and contributing to society. Maslow calls this goal self-actualization, and Thomas Gordon now talks about the integrated person as the ideal. When we are fulfilled by contributing to others, we can experience a "natural high."

During the past twenty years, many teenagers have subscribed to the idea that Libido would give them a feeling of identity and significance, and both males and females have pursued sex promiscuously. However, their only reward in many cases was pregnancy, or V.D.; and at best a very brief sense of belonging to one other person.

Presently, many adolescents behave in the belief that Eros is the sanction for sex. If they are dating each other, and have a meaningful relationship, they feel entitled to explore the sexual content of their commitment, and are willing, however temporarily, to accept responsibility for each other. This becomes sequential monogamy. Teenagers don't "sleep around" unless they have identity problems and seek recognition.

When we grew up, a generation lasted about twenty years. Today, a generation lasts about four years. Each new generation of teenagers has its own set of values and group norms established by their peer group. These are often expressed overtly by their dress and choice of music, established by their peer group heroes. The lyrics of their favourite records often mirror their attitudes and feelings. The Beatles were the first rock group to express the existential viewpoint to the young thinkers who were challenging the established rules of society in the sixties. For example, their song *Eleanor Rigby* expressed existential loneliness.

The Beatles literally swept youth off its restless feet. To teenagers, everything sounded new and different; "their" music and lyrics rock'n' rolled and changed the world. Rock groups emerged from all corners of North America and Europe.

For the first time in history, inexperienced youth identified, and found, a special place in the world. By 1968, the youth counter-culture experienced enlightment heightened by emotionalism, which, from an existentialist viewpoint, was a decisive moment. Youth had always desired transformation, and now the music experience was miraculous. Of course, many young people did not really hear the lyrics; only the "media was the message." Marshall McLuhan hypothesized and proved the point. Their appreciation for and knowledge of the sound, plus their parents' disapproval, became their passport to becoming accepted by their peers. This was the way they achieved the sought-after feeling of belonging, the real reason for them to buy pop records and flow with the "movement" that became antiestablishment. "Do your own thing" became the theme of the youth counter-culture movement.

But it wasn't long before the more intelligent adolescents discovered this wasn't enough. They said to each other, "We must search for more humanistic beliefs and make experience even more meaningful!" Thus, many tried to experience as much as possible, and to cram as much as possible into each experience. They travelled alone or in groups, hitch-hiking not only in North America and Europe as backpackers, but also into Asia to discover the experience of Oriental traditions.

Today, a resigned nihilism has settled over youth. The young teenager believes only in the present. The "here and now" is the only purpose for adolescent living, whether it be winning the game, going to the rock concert or being at the party. Today is the time to experience anything worth living. The young mind exploding with the quest for experience decides to refute the intrusion of thoughts about the past and to ignore any fears about the future.

A strong, skillful and educated young person can live in this self-imposed void with the assurance that his learning will sustain him. He believes that he will survive because he has the knowledge to. His existential teachers and his philosophy books have convinced him that he has unique ultimate powers. The weak, less skilled adolescent who wants to get ahead, but buys into the promises of the drug market, the music scene and promiscuous behaviour, often finds himself in trouble with his parents, his work, the law and his friends. So he becomes a nihilist even though his aspirations were great, because his value structure has become so skewed he cannot cope with one or more of what Adler called the Five Tasks in Life. In his despair, his hopes of finding meaning to existence, his sexuality, his achievements in work and his relationships with others will dwindle away. What remains of his self-respect is questionable. He is left asking the age-old questions, "What am I?" and "Why am I here?"

When the young eventually mature or become parents, they may return to their original traditional religions and again practise the accepted social rituals. Each growing person searches and finds his own answers and solutions according to his own interpretation of experience with his own thoughts. However, it is our job to provide the foundation of self-knowledge that will enable him to begin this search.

If our child is artistic he will see the moon from afar and romantically enjoy its presence. If he is scientific, he will explore its existence further. If he is an idealist, he will reach for it. If he is adventurous he will want to travel to it. If he is insane he will want to live on it. If he is an existentialist, he will jump over it. If he has a feeling of belonging to the earth he will return with increased knowledge to live and be happy to enjoy what is, and contribute to others.

1
Life-Style Analysis

Many advertisers attempt to convince us that our life-style is evident from our choice of home, neighbourhood, club, restaurant, friends, work, entertainment, food, beverage or cosmetic. This erroneous use of the term life-style is a mere strategy of the commercial world, which tries to persuade the consumer that he can elevate his self-esteem and status by buying the advertised product.

What is really meant by the term "life-style"? What is the original definition? The first person to use this term was Alfred Adler, in 1910. He developed the humanistic theory of personality, and stated as its major tenet that life-style is—

1. one's style of acting, thinking, perceiving.

2. one's set of convictions about personal behaviour and life meanings.

3. the unique law of movement for each individual—toward success or toward trouble.

Adler also claimed that all behaviour is purposive movement toward a specific goal. The goal designed by the individual may be constructive or destructive and will be part of the life-style of functioning.

No life-style typology in itself is negative. It depends on our free will and self-determinism. We can recognize our motivation and use our assets to develop ourselves and help others, or decide to use our self-defeating mechanisms as an excuse to become incompetent and emotionally dependent on others.

One may ask, "Why is it important to analyse a person's life-style?" The answer is that life-style is the point of reference from which we interpret, control or predict experience.

When a person is functioning well and coping with life's problems adequately, knowledge about life-style may satisfy curiosity but is not necessary. However, when a person is under stress and experiencing difficulty in coping with people or work, such information may prove to be very helpful.

In order to assess the life-style of an individual, the following five components are considered:

1. Self-concept—I am (self-image)

2. Self-ideal—I should be (ethical convictions)

3. My view of the world—"It is..." "People are..." (environmental evaluation)

4. My unique strengths and assets

5. My self-defeating mechanisms.

The self-defeaters are the unaware motivations that get a person into trouble. The life-style assessment or analysis is derived from collecting information from the individual's recounting of situations that are remembered from childhood. The counsellor asks the client questions concerning all of the following topics:

1. His family constellation—birth order

2. The personality of each of his parents

3. His memory of what his parents expected of him

4. What he did as a child to get approval from significant adults (parents, relatives, teachers)

5. Early recollections—memories of specific incidents that the client can recall visually, remembering what was said and the feelings that he experienced at the time.

6. Recurrent dreams during his childhood

7. His feelings about his awakening sexuality—his attitude

toward becoming an adult with the ability to reproduce, or even just to perform, with the opposite sex

8. His rating of his abilities in forty different character traits—e.g., sense of humor, aggressiveness, standards of right and wrong.

This information is recorded verbatim and interpreted later.

Parents and teachers who work with young children must realize the tremendously important part that they play in this development. Although children "find their place" in the family according to their relationships with their siblings, the adults who care for them provide them with their status by their approval or disaproval of certain behaviours.

Parents, teachers and other adults who work with children over age eight cannot change their life-style, but *can* help the person change from using his life-style typology in negative ways to using it positively. This process involves the adult changing his role from being a child-trainer to becoming an adolescent's consultant.

A therapist will analyse the life-style of the patient in order to decide the future course of therapy.

Factors that Influence Life-Style*

Heredity:
- The child's "inner" environment, or what he is born with, may account for some tendencies, talents, or interests, but the family environment and social experience have a greater influence on personality.

Family atmosphere:
- Relationship between the parents becomes the basis for the family atmosphere or family climate.
- Attitudes of the parents toward their sex roles.
- Domination of father or mother.
- Submission of father or mother.
- Competition vs. co-operation between father and mother.
- Conformity vs. creativeness.
- Ambition of parents for themselves and their children.
- Mutual respect vs. "smother love."

* Acknowledgement to Mrs. Floy Pepper, Portland, Oregon.

- Order vs. chaos.
- Children encouraged to "be oneself" or to "put up a front" to cover up their true feelings.
- Humiliation; or, are family members treated as one would treat a friend whose friendship one wanted to cultivate? From the atmosphere in his home, the child gets his first experiences in forming his own relationships, attitudes, and concepts.

Family Values:
- What is important to both parents.
- Examples of "family values" education:
  honesty, success, conformity to social norms, health, communication.
- Family values cannot be ignored: each child must take a stand.
- Child may conform or rebel, side with one parent against the other if the parents disagree, but not remain neutral.
- Conforming children usually accept the parents' values.
- Rebellious children "kick" these values, since these are sensitive areas and parents are highly vulnerable.

Family Constellation:
- The interaction between members of the family.
- All would agree that parents affect their children.
- Children also affect their parents.
- Interaction of the siblings is important in development of personality development.
- Most important is the child's own interpretation of his situation, *how he feels about it.*
- Parents are often unaware of how their actions fortify each child's interpretation of his situation, of his *place:*
  - "responsible" child is given more responsibility;
  - "good" child shows up the "bad" one;
  - "baby" has everything done for him so he remains helpless;
  - "real boy", "complete female," "tomboy," "sissy," etc. see themselves in these roles.

It is not what happens to us but how we feel about it.
It is not what we are but what we think we are.
Life is how we see it.

The Beginnings: The Family Constellation

We proceed on the assumption that the way the child interprets his experiences in the family is his major form of reference for perceiving and interpreting and evaluating the world outside the family. The knowledge, habits, and skills that he acquires in the home largely determine his capacity for dealing with outside situations. It is not so much what happens to the child as the way he interprets it that determines his behaviour or movement. His place in the family constellation (see Chapter 10), therefore, becomes very important as a basis of his interpretation. All his strivings are directed towards a feeling of security—a feeling of belonging—so that the difficulties of life will be overcome and that he will emerge safely and victoriously. As Dr. Dreikurs, an educator and psychiatrist from Chicago who was well known for his family counselling, stated, "He develops those qualities by which he hopes to achieve significance or even a degree of power and superiority in the family constellation."

Why Children Are Different

No two children born in the same family grow up in the same situation. The environment of the children within the same family may be different for one or more of the following reasons:

1. With the birth of each child, the situation changes.

2. Parents are older and more experienced.

3. Parents may be more prosperous and own home.

4. Parents may have moved to another neighbourhood.

5. Possibility of step-parent—due to divorce or death.

Other factors which may affect the child's place in the family group are a sickly or crippled child, a child born just before or after the death of another, an only boy among all girls and an only girl among all boys, some obvious physical characteristic, an older person living in the home, or the favouritism of parents toward a child. Adler states, "The dangers of favouritism can hardly be too dramatically put. Almost every discouragement in childhood springs from the feeling that someone else is preferred. Where boys are preferred to girls, inferiority feelings amongst girls are inevitable. Children are very sensitive and even a good child can take an entirely wrong direction in life through the suspicion that others are preferred.''

Adler taught that in the life-pattern of every child there is the imprint of his position in the family with its definite characteristics. He pointed out that it is upon just this one fact — the child's place in the family constellation — that much of his future attitude toward life depends.

2
Birth Order and Personality

What effect, if any, has your order of birth had on your personality? Is there any difference between a first born and middle child, between an only child and the baby? How important is the family constellation?

What makes you the unique individual that you are? How do you cope with life's situations? What methods of problem-solving do you use when life hands you a dirty deal? Where do you find joy, excitement, peace, satisfaction? . . .

You may be thinking, "I am this way because of my heredity, my parents, my genes, my upbringing or my environment." Adlerians believe that throughout life you have made many decisions regarding your own destiny, and no person or situation has *made you* anything that you were not willing to accept. Your perception of yourself, others, life, and the future have always been your guide for your decisions. Life is how we see it. It is not what we are, but what we *think* we are. It is not what happens to us but how we feel about it that counts. Our perceptions and interpretations have determined what we have learned from a situation. Adlerians believe that we are a result of what we have done to others and they have done to us.

All of human interactions that we have been part of have left an indelible print on our personality. We are social beings who want to belong. We are goal-directed in our behaviour.

We are self-determined; we have free will. We are subjective in our perceptions and we are whole beings, neither computers nor robots with compartmentalized boxes of stimulus-response conditioning. Our social learning conditioning has been dependent on our willingness to internalize consequences.

Adlerians describe personality as "life-style." Our true personality is often only apparent when we find ourselves in crunch situations. Usually we function according to our life-styles, at an unaware level. Our life-style may be visible to others but not ourselves. We get confused between our self-concept, which says "I am this" and our self-ideal, which says "I should be that." In the middle of that ambivalence we use "tools" to justify our position. Tools may be our rationalizations, emotions or the placing of blame on others.

Basically, you may be a Getter, a Driver, a Controller, a person who must be Superior, a person who needs to be Liked, a person who needs to be Good, a Victim, a Martyr, a Baby, an Inadequate person, a person who craves excitement, an Aginner, or one who Avoids Feelings.

How and when do we arrive at these personality convictions? We have formed our life-style before the age of eight from our experience of human interactions. The people most important in helping us come to those conclusions were our brothers and sisters, or if we were only children, our play-mates — *not our parents*. The role that our parents played was that of making it all possible.

Birth order or family constellation can be a determining factor in personality. In a co-operative family there are few differences in the children — they all hold the family values (the values important to both parents): religion, education, sports, money, success, honesty, tradition, health, or conformity.

In a competitive family the parents are in conflict and there are greater differences between the children.

For example, the "responsible" child is given more responsibility; the "good" child shows up the "bad" one; the Baby has everything done for him so that he remains helpless, (only-children are most like babies).

To first-borns, Mother serves as a model. First-borns hold mostly to tradition, and are more conservative, more dogmatic, rigid, more conforming and dominating than the other children.

According to research, first-borns feel more responsible for themselves and for society; they are the ones most likely to write autobiographies.

Second-borns tend to be Drivers, and live as if they are in a race with the first-borns as the pace-maker.

Babies and only-children are the most flexible. They are non-conforming and care less about tradition, although they feel most responsible for aging parents.

Also from research, it is found that first-born girls are most likely to indulge in pre-marital intercourse and get pregnant before marriage. Later-borns are more likely to use contraceptive measures and be more secretive about sexual activity. The older girls in a family are experienced babysitters and have watched the younger children develop. Youngest girls are afraid of babies.

What about marriage? Who should marry whom? The most happy marriages, on the basis of research, are unions between first-born husbands and last-born or only-child wives. The wife tends to be happily submissive to the dominant male role. Marriages composed of complementary birth ranks (first-borns married to later-borns) are more successful than marriages consisting of similar birth ranks (first-born married to first-born, later-born married to later-born). These marriages succeed due to complementary needs of personality.

Research by Forer in 1967 and my own research in 1974 concluded that marriages between only-children are very loving relationships as long as the two individuals do not have pampered life-styles. Usually both are grateful for love and companionship and (since they had no siblings) they operate on the basis of a totally giving relationship. They always have more than one child, even if they have to adopt some. They usually decide not to inflict their own children with the loneliness they experienced.

Consider your own children. Do you see them as similar personalities or very different? The more co-operative your marriage, the more similar they are likely to be.

3
Typologies of Birth Order

The Only Child

The only child has a decidedly difficult start in life as he spends his entire childhood among persons who are more proficient. He may feel like a dwarf in a world of giants. He may try to develop skills in areas that will gain approval of the adult world, or he may solicit their sympathy by being shy, timid, or helpless.

Positive qualities often displayed by only-child:

1. Can play alone for longer periods of time than others.

2. Proficient in solving jigsaw and other puzzles requiring independent thought and quiet concentration.

3. Capable of conversing with adults at a level more mature than others. Responds well to a one-to-one relationship.

4. Verbal expression and use of vocabulary above average for his chronological age.

5. An above average amount of information concerning general knowledge.

6. A greater interest in collections, i.e., rocks, stamps, coins, doll clothes, etc.

7. A greater appreciation of order—tidiness, personal hygiene, personal property, sequence and an appropriate place where things belong.

8. A keener sense of what is right and wrong—judgmental.

Difficulties expressed or felt by only-child:

1. Can be a pampered child—overprotected regarding health—catching cold, etc.—safety, eating habits—attention-seeking from adults.

2. If a boy, can have a mother complex, or feel that his father is a rival. A girl may experience the father complex and mother as rival.

3. Can develop an exclusive interest—only in himself.

4. Enjoys a position as a center of interest—possibly in negative ways.

5. Sometimes has a feeling of insecurity due to the anxiety of his parents—They obsessively want him to succeed. He's their only chance of projecting themselves into immortality.

6. Is often taught to gain things by his own effort (not group awareness), is highly competitive and displays the conviction that merely to want something is to have it.

7. If his requests are not granted, he may feel unfairly treated, and refuse to co-operate with others. He feels entitled to any or everything.

8. Is often spoiled with material things, e.g., toys, etc.

Dealing with the Only Child

Since only-children tend to relate well with adults and complete assignments satisfactorily, we sometimes conclude that they have no problems in school. It is more likely that the parents give us the difficulties because of their overambition for the child. At the parent interview it is important that we listen actively to the parents' concerns, assure the parents that the child can function independently, help them to break the apron string ties and point out that the child is possibly lonely and needs friends. We might remember that the single parent possibly smothers the child with love since the family has only two members. The single parent might be encouraged to develop other interests in order to add a healthy perspective to the relationship.

It is likely that the child feels desperately lonely at times. We may assume that if we give lots of personal attention the child will feel better—but this is not true. The child needs to interact more with his peers in the class and the playground. We should extricate ourselves from continually being drawn into a one-to-one relationship, which the child can manage well, and teach him the skills of sharing, listening to other children's feelings; saying and doing truly friendly things, and to avoid showing off or talking about all the expensive things he has. He can also be taught that good friends cannot be bought. In group work he should be placed with extroverted socially mature children who can, by example, show him how friends work and play together. In a classroom atmosphere based on mutual respect, an only child can quickly sense a feeling of belonging and being an important member of a group. In these ways we can prevent, avoid or correct misbehaviour in only children.

The First Child

The first child has a threatened position in life; his being the oldest should entitle him to the favoured spot, and frequently does. However, he may become discouraged upon the birth of the second child, and refuse to accept responsibility. He—

1. is an only child for a period of time and has therefore been the centre of interest.

2. has to be first—in the sense of gaining and holding superiority over the next children.

3. becomes a "de-throned" child with the birth of the second child. (He sometimes feels unloved and neglected. He usually strives to keep or to regain his mother's attention by positive deeds; when this fails, he quite often switches to the useless side and may become obnoxious. If his mother fights back, the child may become a problem child.)

4. could develop a good, competent behaviour pattern or become extremely discouraged.

5. sometimes strives to protect and help others in his struggle to keep the upper hand.

6. sometimes death wishes or expressions of hate are directed toward the second child.

7. If the child is a boy followed within a short time by a sister —

   a) personal conflict may become a pattern of sexual discord.

   b) girls develop faster than boys during ages one to seventeen and press closely on the heels of the first child.

   c) the boy usually tries to assert himself because of social preference for boys and may take advantage of his masculine role.

   d) the girl may develop a feeling of inferiority and overcompensate by being bossy.

The Second Child

The second child has somewhat of an uncomfortable position in life and usually takes a driving attitude, trying to catch up with the child in front and feels as though he is under constant pressure. He —

1. never has his parents' undivided attention.

2. always has in front of him another child who is more advanced.

3. feels that the first child cannot be beaten, which disputes his claim of equality.

4. often acts as though he were in a race; hyper-active and pushy.

5. is more likely to feel uncertain of himself and his abilities if the first child is successful

6. usually is the opposite of the first child. (If the first child

is dependable and "good," the second may become undependable and "bad.")

7. becomes a "squeezed" child whenever a third child is born.

The Youngest Child

The youngest child has quite a peculiar place in the family constellation and may become a "speeder," because he is outdistanced, and become the most successful; or he may become discouraged and have inferior feelings. He—

1. is often like an only child.

2. usually has things done for him—decisions made, and responsibility taken.

3. usually is spoiled by the family.

4. finds himself in an embarrassing position—is usually the smallest, the the weakest and, above all, not taken seriously.

5. may become the "boss" in the family.

6. either attempts to excel over his brothers and sisters or evades the direct struggle for superiority.

7. may retain the baby role, and place others in his service.

8. often allies with the first child as being different from the rest.

The Middle Child of Three

The middle child of three has an uncertain place in the family group, and may feel neglected; he discovers that he has neither the privileges of the youngest nor the rights of an older child. He—

1. may feel unloved or abused.

2. becomes a "squeezed" child whenever a third child is born.

3. may hold the conviction that people are unfair to him.

4.   may be unable to find his place in the group.

5.   may become extremely discouraged, and more prone to become a "Problem" child.

Middle Children — large family

Children who come in the middle of a family usually develop a more stable character, and the conflict between the children tends to be less fierce. In other words, the larger the family, usually the less the conflict and strife among the children.

Generalizations

Every brother and sister has some pleasant feelings and some unpleasant feelings about each other. They are likely to have pleasant relations when they satisfy one another's needs. Since each child feels differently toward each brother and sister, the relationship of any two of them is very special. "As each member strives for his own place within the group, the competing opponents watch each other carefully to see the ways and means by which the opponent succeeds or fails. Where one succeeds, the other gives up; where one shows weakness or deficiencies, the other steps in. In this way, competition between two members of the family is always expressed through differences in character, temperament, interests and abilities. Conversely, the similarity of characteristics always indicates alliances. Sometimes, the two strongest competitors show no sign of open rivalry, but rather present a close-knit pair; nevertheless, their competitive striving is expressed in personality differences. One may be the leader, the active and powerful protector, while the other may lean and get support by weakness and frailty. There are cases where strong competition did not prevent a mutual agreement, but rather permitted each to feel secure in his personal method of compensatory striving."

If there is quite a number of years between the birth of the children, each child will have some of the characteristics of an only child. Perhaps there will be two families — one set of children, then a space of years, then another set. Whatever combination may exist first, with the space of years, the situation changes and shifts, but basically the above characteristics remain the same.

The development of an only girl among boys or of an only boy among girls presents a ticklish problem. Both usually tend to go to extremes—either in a feminine or masculine role. In most cases, both would be somewhat isolated and have mixed feelings and emotions. Whichever role seems to be the most advantageous will be the one adopted. Adler discussed the "will to power" in 1905 by stating:

"Every difficulty of development is caused by rivalry and lack of cooperation in the family. If we look around at our social life and ask why rivalry and competition is its most obvious aspect—indeed, not only at our social life but at our whole world—then we must recognize that people everywhere are pursuing the goal of being conqueror, of overcoming and surpassing others. This goal is the result of training in early childhood, of the rivalries and competitive striving of children who have not felt themselves an equal part of their whole family."

The child's position in the family shows how he uses his situation and the resulting impressions to create his style of life.

4
Typologies of Life-Style*

Since our life-style develops from our interpersonal relationships in our childhood, it is relatively fixed unless we commit ourselves to personal growth in adult life. Growth may take place during therapy, personal trauma or a deeply meaningful friendship.

The following fourteen typologies are descriptions, or oversimplifications. No individual is an exact type. No type is wrong or totally negative. We can use any one of our basic typologies negatively or positively. Negative use gets us into trouble. As we develop positive attitudes toward others, our life-style can be reconstructed toward social interest. Here I describe the negative aspects, in order that you may catch yourself and decide to change, also to help you understand your mate, relative, friend, or client.

The "Getter"

He feels *entitled* to receive and finds it difficult to give. His thought is always, "What's in it for me?" He may be charming but he is usually a passive, dependent individual who is

---

* *Developed by Dr. Harold Mosak and Dr. Bernard Shulman of the Alfred Adler Institute of Chicago. The fourteen basic typologies listed here were first published in* Basic Applications of Adlerian Psychology *by Edith Dewey*, (Coral Springs, Florida: MTI Press, 1978).

not self-reliant. His outlook on life is pessimistic and he often feels that life is unfair to him. He is usually gregarious but he may exploit and manipulate others by putting them into his service. He may use temper, charm, shyness or intimidation as methods of operation. Sometimes he retreats into depression. Some cover up their basic pessimism by a super optimism to assure themselves that "all is fine" or "my luck is bound to change." How did a Getter develop? From interactions with parents and siblings before he was age eight. He was probably taught to "get" and rewarded for little investment. He may have been spoiled by overindulgent parents or has learned to fend for himself by lying, cheating and stealing because he felt neglected.

Some parents want to do everything for their children and give the child the impression that love is contingent upon receiving gifts. Thus every day is Christmas or something is wrong. The child learns at an early age to put others into his service and does not learn to solve his own problems. He may be encouraged to give back information but not to think for himself.

Getters may have been neglected children and spend the rest of their lives trying to get even. Criminal behaviour is often the result. This person needs to be taught the joy of giving. We have found that the pampered child often displays characteristics similar to that of the neglected child.

The "Driver"

He is an active, aggressive, forceful individual who always wants to be first, be on top, be better than others or be the center of attention. He has to win and when he doesn't, he claims he was cheated. He must have his own way, and power is important in all his relationships, although he also feels he would like to please everyone. He believes it is important to be a "real man." His over-ambition is counter-phobic, for underneath he fears he is nothing. A woman Driver wants to be a "real woman."

Many were oldest children who struggled to maintain their superior position. Others may have been the youngest who learned to gain center stage. They usually come from highly competitive families.

Drivers are often second borns who live in overdrive, with the first-born, the perceived pace-maker, out front. They live life as if they are always in a race with the first-born ahead of them.

In order to help the Driver, we must caution him to slow down, relax and feel OK about himself even when he is doing less. These people are prime candidates for ulcers, heart attacks and addictions. They push themselves to their limits and sometimes extend themselves beyond their physical strength. They must learn to relax.

The "Controller"

He either wants to control life or ensure that life will not control him, so he is interested in security. He approaches life with a hesitating attitude, since his goal is that of perfection and he constantly tests himself and life. He needs guidelines for everything, so routines, schedules, order and rules appeal to him. He is overconscientious, punctual, and concerned with cleanliness, neatness and correct dress. He is afraid of his feelings and favors intellectualization. He deprives himself of spontaneity, dislikes surprises and finds it difficult to relax and have fun. He may have good superficial relationships with people. He often criticizes others, thereby exalting himself. He may develop passive methods of controlling others, using tears ("water power") weakness, shyness and charm.

In childhood, there are probably high standards, stress on rewards and punishment, competition, on being more perfect than he was, and he was probably told, "Control yourself." Although discipline was probably strict, the parents did things for him unduly. He learned to cover up his true feelings, developed rituals and kept life at a distance.

Many teachers are Controllers. They believe in their ability to control children, because adults would give them a harder time. The positive use of this life-style is to work at controlling oneself; therefore, self-discipline is a rewarding challenge to them.

In order to help a Controller who is experiencing difficulty in his attempt to control others, we teach him to relax and that spontaneity is not always harmful—some risks are profitable. "Living can be fun!" "All work and no play makes Jack a dull boy."

The Person Who Needs to Be Right

He is an over-ambitious perfectionist with excessively high standards. In the extreme, he may be obsessive-compulsive or become a health-food fanatic. He cannot tolerate ambiguity and needs guidelines for everything. He has trouble making up his mind and may ask for advice to an extreme degree. He is usually in a state of turmoil although he tries to "go by the book." Right and wrong are the all-important issues; if he doesn't know what is right, he doesn't act. He is overwhelmed by the importance of the reactions of other people. He scrupulously avoids error but if caught in error, he rationalizes that others are more wrong than he.

He usually comes from a home with excessive discipline and where high moral standards, success and intellectual correctness were stressed. Power struggles may have occurred between his parents, with each criticising and deprecating the other. This taught him how important it is not to err.

Many scientists and mathematicians function this way, as well as teachers of these specific subjects. We can help a "righter" who is having trouble socially, by teaching him that to be a seventy percenter is good enough to make it in real life situations.

Disraeli, prime minister of England, said, "It is more easy to be critical than to be correct." Teach him to live with reality, to develop skills and to be accepting of others. Teach him to make friends by trusting others.

The Person Who Must Be Superior

He always feels inferior unless he is in a superior position. He functions within the superiority-inferiority syndrome. He strives for significance but has a basic feeling of insignificance. Then he tries to "get even." He has little feeling for others although he uses them as stepping stones for himself. He is vain, frequently rude, and arrogant, although he may maintain a demeanour of politeness that is not genuine. He denies his true feelings, may act "tough" and is defensive. Some have to be master of everything, while others emphasize keeping themselves under control and being above re-proach. He may achieve the record for the number of days of underground burial. He won't enter a life-arena unless he can be the "center" or "best." If he can't be first or best, he may settle for last or worst.

Situations that foster this attitude include those of a pampered child who has others do things for him, or parents in a conflict so that he gets the idea that power is important. Ridicule by parents or other children or keen competition from siblings give him the feeling that he must always stay ahead as do extreme punishment and exposure to inaccurate values (such as "men have to be tough").

This person must learn to see the values in others. Values-clarification exercises in group situations may help. For his own development he should learn to have the courage to be imperfect; then he will feel the freedom to be more sympathetic toward others.

The Person Who Needs to Be Liked

Evaluations of others are the yardsticks of his worth. He depends on the approval of others and is uncomfortable without constant praise. He is extremely sensitive to criticism. Because he is dependent on what is expected of him, he cannot be sincere. He cannot be a strong leader or an efficient boss or be effective in a catastrophe because he might be criticized.

He probably worked only for rewards as a child. When a child is not given a chance to evaluate himself but depends on the evaluation of others, he may seek constant approval. He asks for approval before doing anything. (This is frequently regarded as desirable behaviour.) Parents with high moral standards may make a child who depends upon their approval feel guilty because of his unworthy thoughts. Many parents stress the importance of being liked. They may fear that they might lose the child's love if they discipline him.

This person often becomes a human doormat because he feels that he must play a servant role. This person needs assertiveness training and positive self-concept building and re-inforcement.

The Person Who Needs to Be "Good"

He is a self-righteous person who looks down on others by pointing out their weaknesses. He may advertise his own goodness and seek approval as a reinforcement that he is indeed good, but the approval of others is not sufficient because he himself must feel he is good. His own feelings are more important than the opinions of others. He uses his own standards to determine what "good" is and these standards may be even higher than God's (God can forgive but he cannot). Frequently the wife of an alcoholic is a woman who needs to be "good."

"Goodness" is usually in contrast to the behaviour of someone else. When one child in the family is naughty, another child (usually the one next older or younger) is a "model" child. The goodness of the one provokes the other to be "bad." One who needs to be "good" and becomes discouraged may become extremely "bad."

Teach the person to get off his morally righteous high-horse. He must learn to forgive and forget, to unburden himself of the grudges he continually carries around. Teach him to do his best and then let the chips fall where they may.

The "Victim"

Sometimes called the schlimazel, he is the one who always gets the dirty end of the stick. He is a disaster-chaser and is accident-prone. He sees life as abusive and full of suffering and tragedy. Although suffering is his goal, he is completely oblivious that it is he who provokes his own downfall. He may actually be a courageous person but he sees himself as always losing out and seeking pity. He is pessimistic about life and constantly complains about what is happening to him.

He probably had some unhappiness early in life and got some satisfaction, attention and glory from the pity he received when people felt sorry for him.

Victims habitually put themselves in the losing position. They buy "lemon" cars, then continually complain about them. They leave things to the last minute and procrastinate—then accuse the world of being unfair. Misery seeks misery, so their friends are losers, too. Their common pastime is passing the crying towel. Teach the Victim to use logic, believe in consequences and construct new behaviours. Empathize but don't sympathize.

The "Martyr"

While the Victim merely dies, the Martyr dies for a cause. The Martyr has more arrogance than the Victim; the Martyr feels that he is good and has value. His goal is to suffer and thus ennoble himself and elevate himself above others. But nobility often means no ability. He is highly critical, self-righteous and has high moral standards. He may complain bitterly or be cheerful, playing to his own audience but always feeling sorry for himself. He is an "injustice collector." Some martyrs advertise their suffering; others endure and suffer silently.

Teach the Martyr that suffering is self-defeating behaviour. Tell him that even though the situation is bad, no amount of suffering will improve it.

The "Baby"

He finds his place through charm, cuteness and the exploitation of others. He feels small, weak, helpless and unable to take care of himself. His goal is to get others to serve him. He may ask questions, seek help, try to be the center of attention and expects special privileges. He is dependent on others and wants to be loved or pitied. His voice may remain high pitched and childlike and he may continue to talk "baby talk."

Usually he was the youngest in the family constellation and was not expected to do things for himself. He gave up putting forth effort but developed his charm through shyness, weakness and friendliness in a passive way and thus gained undue attention.

This trait was at one time highly acceptable in women, i.e., the "southern belle," but most women do not favour that behaviour in modern society.

In order to help the Baby, don't fall for the demand for service. Give specific instructions about how to cope with difficult situations. Avoid pity because if you pity him, then he will have justification to feel sorry for his dilemmas, and there is no one more miserable and unwilling to make an effort than some one who feels sorry for himself. Teach him to have confidence in himself and to strive for a sense of accomplishment.

The "Inadequate" Person

This one has an inferiority complex. He feels he is small and weak, that life is difficult and full of trouble or dull and unrewarding. Since he feels he cannot do anything, others should not expect anything from him, nor does he expect anything from himself. His goal is to avoid demands and pressures and he tries to get others to leave him alone. Through his default he indentures others. He avoids responsibility and is threatened by success because he fears that others will then expect more from him. He may be likeable and pleasant but he usually has trouble in an aggressive society. He was probably an underachiever at school, and had particular difficulty in mathematics. He is likely to have difficulty in handling money. Perhaps he was in Special Education.

His parents may have tried very hard to train him properly but they probably had excessive demands for him to get high grades, be good, not fight, not lie, etc. He may have been clumsy and awkward and when responsibility was given to him he would avoid it or fail. He may have come from a famous family and because he was not outstanding he felt he was a failure. Probably he had a high-achieving sibling.

Teach him now to accept responsibility by giving him responsibility. Teach him how to manage money and how to cope in social situations.

The Person Who Craves Excitement

He revels in commotion, feels rules are restrictive and ordinary life and routines are dull. He finds fun in breaking rules and flirting with danger, often bites off more than he can chew, leaves everything until the last moment, makes "messes," does things he should not do. He confuses others and becomes confused himself. He may feel that he is someone special but there is considerable pessimism in his outlook on life. He is often attracted to inappropriate persons. Sex may be used to stir up excitement.

Some homes have lots of excitement and lack of order. Sometimes the parents fight and the children learn various ways to stir up a commotion to attract attention or to distract it. Frequently the youngest child does not want to be left out and finds he can have excitement defending himself.

Teach this individual that life is not a roller-coaster. Being on a high all the time is impossible and the lows become depressing, especially when he has to cope with the trouble he has created. Teach him to control his behaviour—think first. Teach the potential dangers of stirring up excitement and commotion. With teenagers, emphasize the facts of V.D. and the consequences of defying the law.

The "Aginner"

He opposes everything and knows only what he is against. He does not stand for anything. He may be actively against or he may behave passively, circumventing the demands of others. He is an extreme pessimist.

As a child, he was probably "mother deaf" and did not participate in life or make decisions in a constructive way. He probably lacked creativity and spontaneity and was not trained in active problem-solving. Probably he used goals of passive or active power or violent passivity.

Teach him to listen to others, to appreciate their opinions, to keep his mouth shut and try to understand before attacking. Teach him to respect majority rule but if he has a grievance, to present an appropriate proposal.

The Person Who Avoids Feelings

He feels that reason can solve all problems, prizes the rationality of mankind and the intellectual process; he "talks a good game." He fears his own spontaneity, lest he move in a way that he had not preplanned.

In some homes that are "puritanical," feelings are suspect. In others, parents dictate to their children the "proper" feelings for them to have. Sometimes a child observes siblings who express their feelings openly get into trouble and, hence, avoids this. Teach him to touch others, to tell jokes, to appreciate the feelings of joy, sadness and merriment that enrich life.

Adler stated, "As long as a person is in a favourable situation, we cannot see his style of life clearly. However, when a person is confronted with new situations and difficulties, the style of life appears clearly and distinctly."

Dreikurs said, "The style of life is comparable to a characteristic theme in a piece of music. It brings the rhythm of recurrence into our lives."

This short explanation of what Alfred Adler meant by lifestyle is written to help the reader understand the concept. However, a little knowledge can be a dangerous thing. Care and discretion must be used in applying this information to self or others.

Chart 1

Suggested templates for sibling ratings & general life-style themes

Life-style Theme	Rated themselves *Most* when compared to other siblings		
Getter	Selfishness Having own way	Temper tantrums Materialistic	Rebellious Sensitives
Driver	Hardest worker Critical of others	Best grades Idealistic	Standards of accomplishment
Controller	Critical of others Rebellious	Intelligent (Least) Spontaneous	Having own way Standards of accomplishment
Need to be right	Critical of others	Trying to please Best grades	Sensitive easily hurt
Need to be superior	Selfishness Temper tantrums Idealistic	Strongest Attractive	Most athletic Having own way
Need to be liked	Trying to please Considerate	Punished Conforming Attractive	Help around house Sensitive easily hurt
Need to be good	Conforming Hardest worker	Most athletic Idealistic	Critical of others Standards of accomplishment
Aginner	Rebellious Spoiled	Temper tantrums	Sensitive- easily hurt
Victim	Idealistic	Punished	Sensitive- easily hurt
Martyr	Trying to please	Sensitive- easily hurt	Idealistic Punished
Baby	Having own way Attractive	Selfishness Spoiled	Temper tantrums
Inadequate person	Trying to please (Low) intelligence	Sensitive- easily hurt	(Low) standards of accomplishment ...
Avoids feelings	Intelligent	Standards of accomplishment	Best grades Comforming
Excitement seeker	Sense of humor Rebellious	Spoiled Selfishness	Spontaneous Idealistic

Eckstein, Daniel and Baruth, 1975

Chart 2

Decision making

A recent study of adolescent students suggested that there are a variety of personal decision-making strategies commonly used.

Compliant
This person prefers to let someone else decide for him/her. "Whatever you say, sir."

Delaying
This person can't make up his/her mind to decide. "I'll do it later. What's the big rush?"

Fatalistic
This person thinks that what will be will be, so why decide. "It's all in the cards."

Planning
This person is an organized decision-maker who carefully weighs alternatives before deciding. He/she follows a definite strategy.

Impulsive
This person decides and afterwards thinks about the decision.

Agonizing
This person searches for so much information that the decision get so complex, he/she is "lost in the confusion."

Intuitive
This person uses more feeling than thinking. "It feels right inside so I think I'll do it." This is a mystical choice.

Adolescents benefit from being taught the following logical decision-making process:

Paralysis
This person knows he/she must decide but is so overwhelmed by the choices that he/she is unable to make any decision at all.

Logical
Decision making

1. Define the problem.
2. List the alternatives.
3. Identify the criteria, including personal values.
4. Evaluate the alternatives with the criteria.
5. Determine the best alternative but consider consequences.
6. Make the decision.

5

The Human Touch in Today's Educational Climate

Most of our teachers have used one of three teaching styles. The traditional *autocratic* style was harsh, punitive and inhuman, but in the sociological setting of the time, it produced some good results. *Laissez faire-anarchic permissiveness*, introduced in the sixties, was unstructured, disorderly and resulted in little learning. It lead to the adoption of the philosophy labelled "Do your own thing"; unfortunately, many students had insufficient skills to do their own thing with a feeling of competency or a sense of accomplishment. Only a minority found their individuality and became creative.

I suggest that the *democratic* style is the most conducive to learning for all students. It is also the most appropriate style for our democratic society. We are politically democratic, but not democratic in the way we structure our families and schools. We need to train children, even at the elementary level, in the skills of participatory decision-making and problem-solving and not dictate or let them drift.

The democratic teacher is a leader who motivates children to learn what they need to learn—which in the primary grades is the three R's. The democratic teacher influences, stimulates, wins co-operation, guides, and encourages. Respect for order is instilled. The democratic teacher is not afraid of standardized testing. By using the democratic approach he usually finds his students progress much faster, and the test results help in future programming.

This approach was first described by Alfred Adler, who was also the first to develop and practise group therapy. The human touch was introduced into the educational environment by Adler. He stated that we should educate the whole child— the *gestalt*—in body, mind, sensitivity, and spirit.

Children cannot be understood by merely analysing specific test results. The whole child, the *gestalt* encompassing the physical, emotional, cognitive and the spiritual, is greater than the sum total of the parts. Teachers must realize that as children learn academic skills they also learn to cope with the Five Tasks of Life (see Chapter 7).

Adler described the most important trait for teachers to foster as *Gemeinschaftsgefuhl*, or Social Interest. In order to live a meaningful and healthy life in a democracy we must understand that equality implies mutual respect, i.e., concern and love for our fellow man. We must stop thinking in terms of superiority and inferiority and look for our similarities, our connectedness, our common human needs and qualities. Then we can all live in peace without the aggression that violates compassion, empathy and human dignity—while still respecting individual differences.

Also arising in the sixties was the confusion between androgogy and pedagogy. Adults learn best by androgogy. They are experienced, self-directed, independent learners because they have acquired the necessary basic skills. Children learn best by pedagogy because they are dependent learners. The teacher provides the model—the status-forming agent—and motivates the young child to learn what he ought to learn. In the primary grades these are not only the basic skills, the Three R's, but also the Five R's; Respect, Responsibility, Resourcefulness, Responsiveness and Reason. (Reason involving problem-solving and decision-making is probably the most important life skill.)

Curiosity alone is not enough to motivate the child to seek the information that he needs. In order to become a proficient reader, accurate in computation and expressive language, he must be taught in the correct sequence.

The teacher clears the air to keep the classroom invigorating. The teacher is the motivator, the facilitator, the program designer and the loving human model in the primary class-room. In more senior grades, the teacher is still the program designer but enlists the co-operation of the students to participate in decision-making, shared responsibility, setting positive goals for self, and group improvement.

How can we achieve this? First, the teacher must have sensitive communication skills, self-awareness and empathy for others. The teacher must be an encouraging person, because students need encouragement as much as plants need water. The teacher needs to know how to motivate, how to teach skills methodically and sequentially, how to earn respect, how to give recognition to all students, how to integrate a class so that there are no isolates, and how to conduct meaningful class discussions in which students learn to become effective problem-solvers and realistic decision-makers.

Democratic Teaching

What creates an optimum balanced educational climate conducive to an exciting learning environment? The answer is democratic teaching in a controlled programmed atmosphere, and the teacher must express the human touch.

Here are my ten 'human touches' that will help you to create more harmonious climate:

1. Smile and greet the children pleasantly.

2. Use physical touch to emphasize and encourage.

3. Wave at the students in the community from the car.

4. Show a willingness to listen to real problems and to help solve them.

5. Call a student's home to tell parents how *well* their child is co-operating or learning.

6. Ask a student to explain his behaviour before reprimanding him.

7. Try to stand in a child's shoes. Hear with his ears and see with his eyes.

8. Watch life in the classroom by growing plants, fish, small mammals, hatching eggs, etc.

9. Have children make cards and gifts for parents and friends.

10. Show unqualified respect for all children.

Ground Rules for a Democratic Classroom

1. Order is necessary under all circumstances, even in a democratic setting. A group cannot run democratically without order and ground rules.

2. Limits are necessary. School rules and school policies may not be acceptable, they may need revision, but, as long as they exist, they must be followed. They are reality.

3. The children must participate in establishing and maintaining the rules necessary for functioning in an orderly group.

4. The group needs leadership and the teacher needs to know how to exert democratic leadership.

5. Without trust and faith in each other a class cannot function democratically. It may require constant efforts to establish mutual trust between students and teacher.

6. The teacher must know how to win the co-operation of the students. He cannot demand it.

7. A spirit of co-operation has to replace competitiveness in the classroom.

8. A classroom atmosphere conducive to learning co-operation and mutual help is essential for solving problems through democratic transaction.

9. The teacher needs the skill to integrate the class for a common purpose; each child has to have a sense of belonging to the whole class.

10. The pattern of relationships existing in a class is usually established during the first few days. It requires the full attention of the teacher to give each child a feeling of belonging.

11. Group discussion is essential in a democratic setting. It does not consist of chit-chat, but of listening to each other, understanding each other, helping each other, and solving the common problems in the classroom.

12. The democratic school setting requires class and school councils in which all segments of the school population are represented.

6
Child Training

In autocratic classrooms, the child learned that power, prestige, and profit are the only values that count; this produced a
rebellion. The goal of our new democratic tradition is to train
children to be co-operative and happy to contribute.

I feel we need to learn to see with the eyes of a child, hear
with his ears, and stand in his shoes. We can then understand
more about motivation and more about learning.

When we have good days, we should ask ourselves, "What
did I do right today?" and learn from our successes. When
dealing with misbehaviour we should separate the deed from
the doer, the act from the actor. Accept the child but not the
behaviour.

We look at the child as a social being who wants to *belong.* As
long as he is not discouraged and is sure of his worth, his desire
to belong will express itself by his willingness to look at the
situation as it is, and to do what is supposed to be done about it.
Some people believe that children should learn what they want
to learn. Not so! For the child's good mental health, he should
be motivated to learn what he ought to learn—which in primary grades is the basic skills of reading and mathematics, and
how to socialize appropriately in a group.

Logical consequences

Dr. Dreikurs dedicated forty years of his life to helping families and teachers to understand the problems of children, and to improving child-adult relationships. He published 200 books and papers and lectured in many parts of the world. His most popular book for parents is *Children: The Challenge.* I would like to share with you a couple of Dreikurs' stories. This one illustrates how some of our children have become mother deaf—or teacher deaf—*because we talk too much.*

A little girl was playing on a sidewalk in front of a house. Suddenly a window was flung open and a woman called out, "Mary, it's time for supper." The little girl continued skipping. Later the window was opened again and the same woman again called, "Mary, supper is ready." The little girl took no notice. Dreikurs went up to the little girl and said, "Hello, is your name Mary?" "Yes," she replied. "Well, was that your mother?" "Yes," she answered. "Well, why didn't you go in for supper?" Mary then said, "Mother hasn't called three times yet." Yes, we *train* our children not to listen or respond the first time. By giving directions only once we can retrain these same children to listen once and then act. Because mothers who are undergoing retraining will refuse to call twice, a few suppers will be eaten cold, or may be removed because the child is late. But an empty stomach for a few hours is not going to impair the child's health, and will certainly save years of frustration and waste of voice in the future.

If we learn to keep our mouths shut, we can learn anything. We *can* decide to give directions only once and then be quiet. Giving extra service is not training.

Take the story of Frank, a nine-year-old boy who liked to play all the time. He saw no reason to do chores, help around the house, or take responsibility—his mother did it all for him. Dreikurs suggested to this mother the following plan. She was to ask the boy if he would like a day when she would not ask him to do anything—he could do whatever he wanted. He said, "Great. That was a fantastic idea." "But," mother said, "on that day I will do whatever I like, too." He readily agreed. The day arrived. The boy got up. "Where are my pants? What happened to my socks?" he shouted. Mother was still in bed. She answered, "I didn't feel like washing and ironing today." He scrambled to find something to wear, then appeared in the kitchen. "Where's my breakfast?'' ''Oh, I don't feel like getting up this morning,'' mother called. He found something to eat, then muttered as he went off to school. He came home shouting, ''What's for lunch?'' But mother wasn't there. After school he found his room in the mess he had left it in the morning, no supper cooking and his mother enjoying a coffee with the neighbour. ''Where's my library book and my hockey stuff?'' he moaned. Mother ignored him. He was furious. It had been a hard day for both of them. But for the first time in his life this boy learned that order is for everyone's benefit including his, and he was much more willing to co-operate after that.

This is an example of logical consequences being used as a training device in place of punishment.

The only children who respond to punishment are those who don't need it; they are the ones with whom you may reason. For those who change as a result of punishment, it is at best only a temporary result, and the next day you have to punish them again. But there is something much worse hidden in punishment. When you punish children you imbue in them the conviction that power is all that counts. Consequently, they think, ''If you have the right to punish me, then I have the same right to punish you.''

Rewards and punishments were necessary in an autocratic setting. Both are obsolete today.

When you give the child a reward, he doesn't consider that as the expression of a generous authority. No! When you give him one reward he won't bend another finger unless you give him another award. And neither will his classmates volunteer unless they also get a reward.

So how do we train?

Presently we spend more time, money and tears over one untrained child than we do in actively training a whole class. Do we assume that children come to school with a firm understanding of what it means to be a responsible person, or do we consciously work at it?

If training were as simple as setting a good example, we would not find so many irresponsible children coming from homes and schools where the parents and teachers are responsible.

We must realize we do not teach children how to take on responsibility if *we* take on responsibilities for them.

We have no tradition now to guide us in how to live with each other as equals because it hadn't been necessary until about twenty years ago. Whenever people live together, conflicts of interest are inevitable. But how do we deal with it? When a teacher and child are in conflict the teacher usually does one of two things. He either fights with the child, violates respect for the child, or gives in and violates respect for himself. To what extent should we be permissive? To what extent should we be restrictive? What is better, to be hanged or to be shot? If we are permissive, the children run wild, and they have no respect for us. If we are restrictive and punish them, they punish us back. To solve problems we must avoid both fighting or giving in.

How many of us think about reaching agreement instead of only thinking about winning an argument? Do we know how to extricate ourselves from conflict? Do we know it takes two to fight? Do we use logical and natural consequences, or do we still fall back on useless punishment?

The Four Goals

When we are dealing with a misbehaving child we are dealing with "discouragement." A child needs encouragement as a plant needs sun and water.

If they are discouraged they no longer believe that they can find their place through making useful contributions, so they switch to the useless type of behaviour.

I repeat, when we observe misbehaviour we are observing "discouragement." We must remember that a young child is an excellent observer but a poor interpreter. Since behaviour is goal-directed, and the child depends on adults for his status, his faulty logic may produce mistaken goals about how to be significant. In children under ten years of age, according to Dr. Dreikus, there are only four mistaken goals. In understanding behaviour, don't look for causes; notice what the consequences are. Ask yourself, "What was the payoff for the child?" and you will begin to see the child's faulty logic.

These four mistaken goals are limited and exclusive to young children up to the age of ten. They still can be found in adolescents, but they are not exclusive any more, since other ideas about finding status, particularly with the peer group, have developed. Young children behave in line with one of these four goals: first, they want to get attention. They prefer to get attention in a pleasant way, but if they can't, they don't mind provoking and getting it by being disturbing. When we give attention at the time they demand it, we are reinforcing this mistaken goal. Attention is their way of saying, "That is when I count, when I keep you busy."

If the child is more discouraged he switches to the second goal—power. He thinks, "If you don't let me do what I want, you don't love me." He often says, "I hate you." He feels it is his right to do what he wants, and to have everyone else let him do it. If everybody doesn't do things for him, it's unfair. Whatever you tell him to do, he won't do; and as soon as you tell him what not to do, he feels honor-bound to do it. The fight becomes more intense when the child is no longer interested in attention or power but finds his place only through revenge—Goal Three. His aim is to hurt and punish you as much as he perceives that he feels hurt and punished by you. The child showing Goal Three-type behaviour feels that the world is against him and that he must get his attack in first— hence his hostile behaviour.

Goal Four is illustrated in the deeply discouraged child who simply wants to be left alone. As long as you don't demand anything from him, he feels that his deficiencies will not become known. He believes, "If I don't try I can't fail." "You can't tell me how wrong I am if I do nothing." Thus, criticism is avoided (see Chart 5, p. 91).

Now the sad part is that most adults who try to correct a child do the worst possible thing—namely, exactly what the child expects them to do—reinforce the mistaken goal. When a child wants attention, they go after him, nag him, and talk to him. When he wants power, they tell him, in effect, "You can't do that to me," so he turns around and shows he can.

Nobody who fights with a child wins. When you tell a revengeful child that you are hurt by him, you are reinforcing his mistaken goal. If you say, "I don't know what to do with you. I give up," then you are reinforcing the fourth mistaken goal—display of inadequacy.

In order to know which goal the child is using, you must be sensitive to your own feelings when he misbehaves. If you feel *annoyed* you are likely dealing with Goal One—attention-seeking. If you feel that your authority is *threatened*, it is Goal Two—power. If you feel *exasperated*, ("How mean can he be?") it is Goal Three—revenge; and if you feel like throwing up your hands and *giving up*, it may be Goal Four—the display of inadequacy.

To correct Goal One behaviour, ignore the deliberate, destructive attention-seeking, but give positive attention when the child is co-operative. Catch a kid doing something good. For Goal Two, avoid conflict, and give the child opportunities to use his power constructively. For Goal Three, persuade the child that he is likeable, and do some unexpected kindness for him. For Goal Four, boost his self-concept and help him to develop a feeling that he is worthwhile.

The secret of child training is to know when to talk and when to be quiet. This comes only through giving full unbiased attention to the needs of the situation, assessing behaviour constantly, and not falling for children's mistaken goals. Be healthy, relaxed, confident and consistent. Be positive; accept yourself with your own imperfections. Most important is to develop the skills of being an encouraging person. Build on strengths, not weaknesses, and see something good in every pupil.

There is a Chinese story which accentuates the acceptance of oneself and of life as it is.

There was once a poor Chinese farmer. He had a difficult plot of land to cultivate and only one son and a horse and plow to help him. One day the horse ran away. All the neighbours came to commiserate with the farmer and to deplore his bad luck. The farmer sat quietly and said, "How do you know it is bad luck?" The following week the horse came back with ten wild mares. The farmers then came to congratulate him on his good luck. And the farmer sat quietly and said, "How do you know it is good luck?" A week later, his only son, while riding one of the wild horses, was thrown off and broke his leg. Now the farmer had no one to help him. The neighbours came again to commiserate and deplore his bad luck. Again he sat quietly and said, "How do you know it is bad luck?" A week later a war broke out, and the soldiers came and took all the young men away except the farmer's son who had a broken leg.

The wisdom to this story is that we are not here to judge

good luck, bad luck, success, failure. We don't know what will come. We are here to do our share, to make our contribution and let the chips fall where they may.

We must develop the courage to be imperfect, the ability to accept ourselves as we are, and keep trying.

There are ways to overcome the most difficult situations if we have faith in ourselves and trust in others.

Let us start training our children to live as co-operative human beings now. In other words, let us encourage this natural desire to contribute, learn and share, which is part of the tremendous potential in all of us.

7
Discipline in the Classroom

We must have all wondered why some children behave, do the right thing and learn well, while others do just the opposite.

We know how easy it is to teach a class of well- disciplined students who are ready and eager to learn, and we also know how difficult it is to teach a class where many of the pupils have learning problems, family problems, or behaviour problems.

Even if there is only one discipline problem child in the class, the whole atmosphere is disrupted, and all the children react to the disturbance. We must remember that the disrupter is just as much a problem to the other students as he is to us. And we have a social obligation as well as a survival motivation to do something about it to change him. In order to bring about this change we must first realize that discipline and human relationships are interwoven.

The behaviour of the disrupters is often closely linked to the behaviour of their teachers. To illustrate this I would like to tell you a story about a boy named Jack.

Jack was seven years old, had been disrupting the class throughout the morning and had not completed his assignments. The teacher became quite angry and shouted at him, ordering him to stay in after 3:30 to finish his work. After the class was dismissed, the teacher sat at her desk, working on her day-book, and he sat working at his little table. In due time he finished the assignments, and she told Jack that he could go home. But then she said, "How is it possible Jack, you are such a nice boy here now, and yet you were such a horrible person in the class?" And Jack looked up at her in utter surprise and said, "But teacher, I was just thinking the same about you." You see the implication. In a classroom setting, the teacher appeared to Jack to be just as miserable as she thought he was.

Neither the teacher nor Jack had learned to behave constructively in a group situation. But we teachers can learn new methods, no matter how long we have been teaching.

At one time during the sixties I found myself teaching a very hostile Grade Four class. They had experienced three years of permissive education and had learned very little in the process. Over half of them were reading below Grade Two level and seven of them were at the pre-primer stage. Their Math ability was equally low and very few could write legibly. Their social behaviour was worse. They continually fought, stole, told lies, cheated and argued. I was desperately in need of help. I doubted whether I could survive the year with them.

Fortunately for me, at that crucial time, I met Dr. Dreikurs. He taught me some new techniques to use and I found that they really worked. My feelings about teaching changed rapidly from despair to hope, and then to excitement about the fantastic progress these discouraged children made. They all reached grade level by May and became very creative in art, music and poetry. Their stories were unforgettable. They illustrated two books for a publisher, and designed a record cover for a famous musician. They also made two movies and ten film strips. I was so enthusiastic about their response to the Dreikurs method that I was encouraged to write a book, *Discipline Without Tears*, with Dr. Dreikurs, to help teachers who have problems in classroom behaviour.

We know that teaching is a continuous exercise in human relationships. Discipline is also a two-way street, in which not only does the child's behaviour affect the teacher, but the teacher's behaviour affects the child.

We cannot force children to learn. We can lead a child to education but we cannot make him think. Instead, we must know how to motivate and influence our students to choose to grow in specific constructive directions. Then, in the junior and senior grades they will have the skills with which to do intelligent research and meaningful projects.

Many of our present expensive remedial programmes in the senior schools could have been avoided. Many groups of discouraged youngsters struggle with these basic skills while their friends are enjoying more exciting activities. The Primary department needs strong, well-qualified, highly skilled teachers. I believe that the primary teachers need the smallest classes, as well as an ample budget and due respect for the enormous task they undertake each day.

Primary teachers even have to teach children how to listen. Many children live in very noisy homes with loud record-players and radios. They have watched thousands of hours of TV and have learned how to become mother- and teacher-deaf.

If you have any non-listeners in your class, you might try some old-fashioned techniques that still work. Of course you never start a lesson until you have everyone's attention. But how do you accomplish that? You might smile and say one or more of the following:

1. Good morning, boys and girls.

2. Are we ready?

3. Everything off your desks.

4. Is your chair in the right position?

5. Hands together.

6. All eyes looking at the blackboard screen, modulator, etc.

7. We are waiting for John.

If John takes a long time to settle, you might stare at him, or go and stand by him, but don't talk to him. If a child calls out or disrupts you while the lesson is in progress, stop teaching and say nothing until he settles again. If there is a lot of noise, you ask *all* of the students to put their heads down and think happy thoughts, and feel the beauty of "golden silence."

You might need to train children to understand the meaning of the word *silence*, by doing this for one minute the first day, two minutes the second and so on, till they can manage to sit still and be absolutely quiet for five minutes.

Discipline conditioning techniques such as these can be useful, but a deeper understanding of social behaviour is essential for all of us. We are models in our classrooms, and we know that pupils learn more from a model than from a critic. So maybe we should begin by looking at ourselves. Who are we? What are our values? Why are we teaching? What are we teaching? What are our hopes for the future generation?

No nation of the future needs scientists who are not honest, bright citizens who are not dependable, able men without positive attitudes, or educated youth who do not understand the equality of man.

Through a values-education program we must actively train children to be honest, responsible and concerned about others.

The Five Tasks of Life

The values that I promote are based on the five life tasks developed by Alfred Adler.

1. First, we must learn to get along with ourselves, to enjoy our strengths yet accept our imperfections—and if necessary, constructively do something to gradually improve. There are many books and courses available to help us. Increasing human potential, sensitivity, awareness and self-growth are all topics that we should be exploring. How can we teach a child to grow with self-awareness if we don't understand ourselves?

2. The second task of life is how to get along with others; how to gain and maintain friendships; how to love and accept love, and how to be a loving person. If we feel comfortable about our interpersonal relationships, we will know how to help students who are having difficulties in the socialization process.

3. The third task is the task of work. Everyone needs an opportunity to be creative, to feel the joy of accomplishment, to sense the blissful relaxation of tired muscles. We need to be able to do some kind of work, either for self-gratification or money, or to feel that we have made some valuable contribution to someone or to society.

We cannot teach children to love work if we give them work to do as punishment for misbehaviour. Correctional techniques such as class discussions, encouragement, contracts or logical consequences are more effective and less damaging to the students' concept of life. In fact, some wise teachers deny the child the opportunity to be productive as a logical consequence for inappropriate behaviour. They say, "Since you do not work co-operatively, sit quietly and do nothing." This is most effective with students under ten years of age.

4. Our fourth task in life is to manage our sexuality, i.e., to enjoy this natural activity without exploiting others. This involves the art of happy dating and the skills of marriage and parenting. Those of use who teach adolescents find that many discipline problems develop when teenagers try to attract each other by using acting-out behaviour. They lack co-operative skills, and either spitefully compete or give up and become depressed. Those high schools that teach programmes of communication skills, mutual respect and family life education are experiencing fewer discipline problems. Their students are happier and more productive; they get high on school rather than seeking highs through alcohol or drugs.

5. The fifth task of life is finding a meaning to existence, the cosmos, nature and the balance between man and the environment.

At the junior and intermediate levels we can provide units of work on religions, outdoor education, and pollution to help students appreciate their responsibility to life and feel that they have an integral place in the world. Responsibility is taught by giving responsibility according to the student's maturity and guiding him through increasingly challenging duties. A point to remember is, Never do for a child what he can do for himself.

Revolution

I am sure you must be wondering why we still have so many discipline problems even though we have advanced teaching techniques and well-developed programs.

The problem, as I see it, is a result of sociological evolution. No one prepared us for living in a democracy. For more than 10,000 years we have lived in an autocratic society (except for a brief interlude in Classical Greece).

What we are witnessing today is a rebellion by all those who were previously dominated. They no longer blindly accept the dictates of authorities. The revolt is for participation in decision-making and equality. These desires have been voiced loudly by blacks, women, trade unions and also the poor. They have been heard, and we'll hear more, much more, from those who will overcompensate in their struggle for equality and will then demand superiority.

Few teachers realize that many of our students have joined this social rebellion and are now expecting a certain kind of equality. It's not hard to understand, because historically they have always been treated as inferior to everybody. Mass prejudice against children has been socially acceptable, but now children also crave participation in decision-making. They want a say in matters that concern them.

However, there is no ill produced by democracy that cannot be cured by more democratic training.

Equality is a difficult concept to grasp. We haven't yet learned to live with each other as equals. I believe that this unfortunate ignorance is the cause of most of the troubles that we find in the classroom. Social equality is not implying equality in size, age, position or intelligence, but equal respect. We must have the same respect for a Grade Two child as we have for our grandfather, and the same respect for the clerk in the supermarket that we have for our principal. We need a teaching relationship based on mutual respect, i.e., we respect the students for their human individuality and they respect us. Children today do not automatically respect their teachers. We must earn respect by being knowledgeable and competent.

Mutual respect is the only basis on which to solve problems in the classroom.

Wanted: A New Tradition

In the past, child-raising and education were based on tradition. But where are the traditions in our country today? Most of them have been lost in the revolving wheels of accelerated change. Our culture has changed so rapidly that a generation of students now changes in four years, instead of the eighteen years it took when we were young. We teachers, particularly in high schools, must be constantly aware of the changing values and cultural patterns of youth.

We must be open and receptive to their new ideas, and yet at the same time hold true to our own values and standards, some of which are timeless. However, there is one fact of life that I do think needs changing.

Many parents insist that we must prepare children for living in a competitive society by making competition a part of the curriculum in primary grades. This is unfortunate, because we know from research that the less competitive a person is, the happier he will be and the more able he is to cope well in competitive work situations because he concentrates on his task rather than on what someone else is doing.

Certainly children must be taught to function in society as they find it—which, I admit, is competitive—but we don't have to continue teaching methods that result in a great deal of unhappiness, friction, and non-productivity from discouraged students.

Einstein always taught that "competition brings death for many, and co-operation provides life for all." Co-operation is the key word for a sane and enjoyable class. For example, if a child can't spell, ask for a volunteer who will be willing to help, instead of your doing everything. Children enjoy helping each other. Try to eliminate from your classroom as much competition as you can. Then you'll probably find you have eliminated a lot of discipline problems, too.

There is one more key word to help you to attain a harmonious class, a class you can look forward to teaching instead of dreading.

Participation: every pupil is equal to every other. All the kids get their art on the wall, not just the young Picassos. All boys and girls play on the team or act in the play, not just the budding stars. Participation, not the final score, is the goal. The students all learn, have fun and enjoy contributing.

When children are confident of their skills, and have experienced the joys of co-operation and participation in the family, nursery school and elementary school, they will accept that winning or losing are facts of life, but not the most important.

Here are some rules of thumb for teachers of very young children:

1.   Watch for a child's first attempts to do things for himself or to help you. Encourage these attempts. Give a child credit for trying new things or helping you.

2.   Don't criticize or condemn poor results. Gradually and tactfully steer the child toward better ones.

3.   Realize when a child is ready for advanced learning or greater responsibilities and let him take them on.

4.   Always set tasks that you think the child has a reasonable chance of achieving.

Adler's Five Premises

Alfred Adler taught us that man is always creative and forms his personality from his interactions with others. I would now like to discuss the five premises of Adler's theory. Even though they were formulated many years ago they are still valid and most helpful to us today.

1. We are socially embedded (in contrast to the Freudian theory of a hereditary or biological basis of behaviour): All behaviour problems are basically social problems. We want to belong—to find our place in the group. The group is the field in which we move, even if we move away.

Dr. Dreikurs used to illustrate this point with the story of the hermit. Many years ago, a hermit lived in a cave ten miles from the nearest village. He had lived there for thirty years. One day the village was swept away in a flood and the elders decided to rebuild three miles north on higher ground. A few weeks later the villagers noticed that the hermit had also moved—into another cave, also three miles to the north.

One's ability to co-operate and to contribute serves as a measure of his social interest; the maladjusted person has faulty concepts, feelings of inferiority and mistaken goals. Well-adjusted individuals consider others while assessing and evaluating solutions to problem situations.

The infant first expresses this desire to belong to his mother and father (he finds his place in the family) then to his teacher at school, then to his peer group in adolescent years. We know that this desire to belong is stronger than any other motivation at the teenage stage—greater than love of family, interests, learning—even stronger than the conscience that discriminates between right and wrong. Hence we find street gangs, fashion fads and the drug scene.

2. We are self-determining and creative (in contrast to mechanistic-deterministic theories). We are active participants who not only react—we *act!* We are not victims of our drives. We *decide* what we will do, although we are usually unaware of our decisions. Therefore, we *can* change—this is the basis of our optimism. Negative thinking is destructive, but positive thinking becomes productive.

When we observe an infant, we find that he certainly acts to get what he wants. He cries and finds out he can manipulate his mother to feed, cuddle or entertain him. He attempts to manipulate father in the same way, but is usually not quite so successful because fathers are usually away more often. With an infant born to deaf mutes—it is amazing to see that it only takes four months for him to learn that crying gets him nowhere. The face is in grimaces, the hands clench, tears stream from the eyes, but no sound comes out of the mouth. He develops other creative methods to attract mother.

Children train and manipulate adults!

If you feel offended by the use of the word *manipulation*, start thinking about transactions with misbehaving children. They can manage adults, but the adults can't manage them.

3. We are goal-directed (as contrasted with a casual evaluation of behaviour): Our behaviour is purposive—although we are usually unaware of its purpose. Most efforts to understand people have been directed toward causes, due to the Freudian influence, but the cause of behaviour can only be speculated upon. To understand behaviour, look at its consequences, which are more easily recognized. Causes can't be changed—goals can.

Once a goal is recognized, the child can be offered a choice. He may continue as before (but no longer in innocence, which usually makes not changing less palatable) or he may change, which is encouraging.

Let us consider the psychological technique of spitting in one's soup. You order your favourite soup in a restaurant. Suddenly, just before you are about to enjoy it, someone leans over and spits in it. You feel disgusted, and onion soup never tastes the same again. It feels the same to a child after a confrontation has taken place about his mistaken goals. His behaviour may continue, but it will never feel good again, and so repetition of this behaviour will decrease.

If we try to explain behaviour by causes, there is little hope that the person will change. He will have a new excuse for misbehaving. An alcoholic may rationalize and say, "I am an alcoholic because I have an oral fixation." But if we counsel him and discuss the purpose or intention of the behaviour, that person will think twice before he intends to misbehave by getting drunk again; now he can change his intentions and in future will behave differently.

4. We are subjective in our perceptions. Reality for each of us is dependent on our perception of it, and our perception is likely to be biased or mistaken. We cannot be objective about ourselves and our interpretations of experience. It is not what happens to us, but how we feel about it. Two people can witness exactly the same accident yet report different stories. Their reports will be influenced by how they feel about themselves within that situation, and are quite likely to be in line with their lifestyles.

Our most valuable teaching tool is our awareness and understanding of how a child learns, and the meaning and purpose of his behaviour. Without this skill we cannot influence a child to develop new concepts.

To develop this sensitivity requires much practice, but it is essential if we want to be really effective teachers.

5. A holistic approach is used to observe the child. The whole is more than the sum of its parts. To understand a student we should look at repeated patterns of behaviour, and not only isolated incidents or facts such as I.Q. scores or achievement test results.

These five basic premises and assumptions are true for all people, adults and children.

We look at the child as a social being who wants to belong. As long as he is not discouraged and is sure of his worth, his desire to belong will express itself by his willingness to look at the situation as it is, and do what is supposed to be done about it.

Encouragement

The well-adjusted child has been encouraged by the adults who have nurtured and trained him. He feels significant and worthwhile.

The maladjusted child feels insignificant and useless. He has given up trying to find his place through constructive contribution and switched to destructive behaviour.

When we observe misbehaviour we are observing *discouragement*. A misbehaving child is a discouraged child. We must remember that a young child is an excellent observer but a poor interpreter. Since behaviour is goal-directed, and the young child depends on adults for his status, his faulty logic may produce *mistaken goals* about how to be significant.

In understanding behaviour, don't look for causes but notice what the *consequences* are. Ask yourself, "What was the payoff for the child—what was the goodie?" And you will begin to see the child's faulty logic.

Teenagers misbehave due to their discouragement about not being accepted by the peer group. For adolescents, the peer group is the value-forming agent and they struggle to achieve a sense of belonging—in their dress, music, activities and behaviour.

One of the most powerful methods of helping children to bring about an improvement in their relationships is the process of encouragement. The technique of encouragement is extremely complex. But every child needs encouragement as a plant needs water. As teachers we must learn to be encouraging people. That will help us to preserve our own sanity.

What are the tools of maintaining sanity in a classroom? How can we teachers train children to realize more than the present 15% of their potential? How do we encourage co-operation?

My suggestions:

1. We build on strengths. We recognize our own strengths and those of our students. On your class list write something good about every child. Also take the staff list, including the secretary and the janitor. Find something positive to write about everyone that you work with.

2. We treat everyone with equal respect—the provocative and hostile children in the same way as the co-operative and charming ones.

3. We use the encouragement process. Remember, praise is a bonus for the successful. Encouragement is *essential* when a child makes mistakes.

4. We use logical consequences instead of punishment.

5. We use our sensitivity to gain insight, to help diagnose and treat misbehaviour rather than openly reacting and reinforcing it.

6. We hold a class discussion meeting once a week to solve problems and to encourage participation in decision-making.

7. We as teachers know the importance of a carefully planned program tailored to fit the needs of each student. If a student misbehaves we immediately ask ourselves and the student the basic question—is his program too easy or too difficult? Pupils need to be challenged within their individual potentials.

8. We can use the Instrumental Enrichment* program to elevate the thinking skills of culturally deprived students.

Do's and Don'ts for Healthy Discipline

What can a teacher do in order to have the kind of classroom order which is satisfactory to him and to the students? Are

---

* *Developed and produced by Dr. R. Feuerstein Hadassah-Wizo, Canada Research Institute.*

these two ideals reconcilable? They are, if discipline and order are used as a co-operative enterprise, with understanding on both sides and team spirit. In order to achieve this end, the teacher must know what *not* to do as well as what to do in a given situation.

What can a teacher do in order to have the kind of classroom order which is satisfactory to him and to the students?

1. Avoid preoccupation with one's authority because it may provoke rather than reduce defiance and resistance to learning. The teacher should not be overly concerned with his own prestige. The individuality of each student must be respected at all times.

2. Refrain from nagging and scolding, as this may reinforce mistaken concepts of how to get attention.

3. Do not force a child to promise anything. Most children when frightened will promise to change their behaviour in order to get out of an uncomfortable situation. It is a waste of time because the promise will mean nothing.

4. Do not give material rewards or prizes to the normal student for good behaviour. He may then work only in order to get his reward and stop as soon as he has achieved his goal. What's more, this will only strengthen his belief that he must be paid every time he acts civil or makes a contribution. Recognition for good efforts should be given frequently. Behaviour modification techniques are useful only in severe cases.

5. Refrain from finding fault with the child; it serves no constructive purpose.

6. Avoid double standards, i.e., one for the teacher and another for the student. In a democratic atmosphere, everybody must have equal rights. The teacher should avoid being tardy, doing unnecessary visiting and talking with members of the staff in class when the children are working, or checking papers or doing any kind of work that prevents the teacher from looking at child who is talking to him.

7. Do not use threats as a method of disciplining the child. Although some children may become intimidated and conform for the moment, this method has no lasting value, since it does not change basic attitudes.

8. Do not be vindictive; it evokes resentment and unfriendly feelings.

Let us now consider some of the effective disciplinary measures that a teacher can use.

1. Because problem behaviour is usually closely related to the child's faulty evaluation of his social position, and how he must behave in order to have a place in the class group, the teacher's first concern must be to understand the purpose of his behaviour. Only then will he be in a position to plan more effectively an intervention program for the child.

2. Wait until you have the attention of all class members before you proceed in giving directions—which must be clear and precise.

3. Be more concerned with the future behaviour of the child than with that exhibited in the past. Refrain from reminding the child about what he used to be or do.

4. As soon as a child misbehaves and threatens the general atmosphere in the class, give him the choice of either remaining in his seat without disturbing others, or leaving the classroom.

5. Build on the positive and minimize the negative. There is much good in every child, but if you look only for academic achievement you may never find his true worth.

6. Try to establish a relationship with the child built on trust and mutual respect.

7. Discuss the child's problem at a time when neither of you is emotionally upset, preferably in the regular weekly class discussions.

8. Use natural consequences instead of traditional punishment. The consequences must bear a direct relationship to the behaviour and must be understood by the child.

9. Be consistent in your decisions. Do not change them arbitrarily just because it suits your purpose at that moment. Inconsistency confuses the child as to what is expected of him.

10. See behaviour in its proper perspective. In this way, you will avoid making a serious issue out of a trivial incident.

11. Establish co-operative planning for future goals and the solutions of class problems.

12. Let children assume greater responsibility for their own behaviour and learning. They cannot learn this unless we plan for such learning. Responsibility is only taught by giving responsibility. Be prepared for children to act up at first. Such training takes time.

13. Use the class discussion to set logical consequences for a child behaving in an antisocial manner.

14. Treat the child as your social equal.

15. Combine kindness with firmness. The child must always sense that you are his friend, but should not have to accept certain kinds of behaviour.

16. At all times, distinguish between the deed and the doer. This permits respect for the child, even when he does something wrong.

17. Guide the individual to assume independence and self-direction.

18. Set the behavioural standards and limits from the beginning but work toward mutual understanding, a sense of responsibility, and consideration for others.

19. Admit your mistakes—the children will respect your honesty. Nothing is as pathetic as a defeated authoritarian who does not want to admit defeat.

20. Mean what you say but keep your demands simple and see that they are carried out.

21. Children look to you for help and guidance; give them this security, but make co-operation and self-control the eventual goal.

22. Keep in mind your long-term goal: helping a child become an independent, responsible adult.

23. Children need direction and guidance until they can learn to direct themselves.

24. Close negative incidents quickly and revive good spirits. Let children know that mistakes are corrected and then forgotten.

25. Commend a child when his behaviour shows improvement.

26. Work co-operatively with children to develop a procedure for dealing with infractions of the rules.

27. "Do unto others as you would have them do unto you."

8
Understanding Structure in a Primary Classroom

A good teacher knows three things: (a) how to motivate, (b) how to teach skills sequentially with detailed planning, and (c) how to give recognition. Motivation and loving care are basic ingredients. Capitalize on childrens' curiosity, giving the children a feeling of self worth. Listening skills are essential.

Adequate visual material for presenting skills in reading and arithmetic must be prepared with follow-up activities. Note:

- We hear and forget.
- We see and remember.
- We do and understand.

A teacher must be completely confident in the program he intends to teach. Plans must be reasonable considering the maturity of the pupils. Reasonable production of work must be accomplished daily for continuous progress. Each day, work must be checked by teacher or student and be corrected. Interest and enthusiasm is contagious.

Glasser tells us how to develop a positive identity. We should feel loved and be able to love; then we feel involved. Life is relevant when we are thoughtful of others.

A child must experience success. A sense of achievement produces a success identity.

Discouragement and implication of failure must be avoided.

Children learn more from a model than a critic.

Student and Teacher Needs

A student needs—

1. to feel loved, have a sense of belonging, and to know that he has a place in this world.

2. to feel significant and worthwhile.

3. to have the opportunity to be creative.

4. to contribute and be co-operative with others.

Therefore, a teacher needs to know—

1. how to motivate a pupil to learn.

2. how to teach skills methodically and sequentially.

3. how to earn respect from pupils.

4. how to give recognition to all students.

5. how to integrate a class so that there are no isolates.

... then learning will take place and harmony will exist in the classroom.

Procedure for Promoting a Co-operative Atmosphere

1. Give every child a program that you and he are confident he can handle ... either in the large group, the small group, or in individual tasks.

2. Anticipate probable problems and do everything possible to avoid them. Do the seatwork yourself—note the areas of probable difficulty—cue-teach those areas. Time yourself, then give students a realistic time to complete.

3. Avoid teaching several heavy written work sessions sequentially. Intersperse with music, activity, poetry, etc.

4. Plan in detail.

5. Don't leave students unsupervised unless you are confident that they can function well without you.

6. Expect them to be responsible and creative.

7. Establish routines with the class and maintain them consistently. Any misdemeanor must be dealt with by using logical consequences. Incomplete work must be completed in the student's own time; careless work, rewritten; and corrections made and checked every day. Inappropriate behaviour must be dealt with by the teacher and the class (the principal's office is a last resort).

8. Always stress that students should do their best. Unless there is a health or emotional problem, don't accept less; but teach the courage to be imperfect.

9. Always encourage. Never insult, use sarcasm, or put a student down.

10. Work for class improvement with class graphs or individual graphs.

11. Set projects, book reports, and other assignments with date deadlines that are reasonable. Put dates on the blackboard and train students to copy them down.

12. Provide enrichment every day for fast students. Structure every minute so that there is no time wastage. Have an ample supply of activities and challenging puzzles to stretch the ability of those who complete seatwork quickly.

13. Encourage students to help each other when there is real difficulty; but discourage lazy students from leaning on the more capable and willing helpers.

14. Be friendly, firm and kind, and not a joker setting a "palsy-walsy" tone. Earn respect and they will respect you.

15. Use the class discussion period to solve problems and set new goals.

16. Eliminate unnecessary repetition of instruction or verbal correction. Act, don't talk.

17. Be knowledgeable and confident about your aims, objectives and content, but don't be afraid to refer students to research books. Be positive!

Chart 3

A person needs encouragement   *as*   *a plant needs sunshine and water*

Because OUR BASIC GOAL IS TO FEEL SIGNIFICANT:

We need to experience:—
acknowledgement
affectionate regard
sense of worth
sense of accomplishment
security
feeling of belonging

If these NEEDS are not met we get these behaviours:

withdrawal
revenge
power
undue attention-seeking
feeling of inadequacy
fantasy
competitiveness
learning resistance
anxiety
tension

Some ways to help kids feel SIGNIFICANT:

build on strengths
individual and group counselling
peer teaching
staff education
class meeting

Prepared by Pearl Cassel and Paul J. Kahn, 1977 ©

The Weekly Class Discussion

Group discussions in the classroom are essential. As a group leader the teacher can get important information about the children; their individual problems and their interrelationships. Without class discussions, hostilities may arise that can snowball and produce a miserable atmosphere for students and teacher alike. Group discussions provide the teacher with an opportunity to help the children understand themselves and to change their concepts and motivations.

A classroom discussion—

- minimizes competition.
- promotes responsibility.
- develops self-determinism.
- encourages individuality in a positive constructive way.
- is non-judgmental.
- gives each student a feeling of being listened to.

One period every week should be set aside for this purpose. Here is a suggested format:

Initially teacher is chairperson but individual students can rotate this responsibility. In order to accomplish this, certain rules are formulated, under the teacher's guidance, which can be discussed at the first meeting:

1. Raise your hand if you wish to speak.

When you are invited to speak, stand and make a clear, distinct statement.

2. Listen carefully.

Look at the person who is speaking. Give your undivided attention. Seriously consider the speaker's opinion. (It may be necessary to teach the difference between fact and opinion.)

3. Stick to the point.

Even if you are eager to raise another issue, don't digress from the subject under discussion. An opportunity will come to you later.

4. Don't clam up.

We want to hear from you. Your ideas are valuable, however inadequate you may feel. It is important that you express yourself. Remember—nobody is perfect. We all need the courage to be imperfect.

5. Think together.

There is great power in a group of people thinking and talking about the same thing. We can solve problems and make decisions more effectively. We come to agreement about appropriate classroom behaviour and all of us decide about logical consequences for misbehaviour with young children.

6. Don't insult or put anyone down.

Think positively about every person. We are all individuals having different experiences at home and with friends. How one person sees a situation may be very different from the way you see it. That does not necessarily mean that he is wrong. He may have less information than you, but he is entitled to express his feelings. Grant him that privilege — think and learn that he is a worthwhile person who needs your respect. He may be in a different place than you. Permit him to have that place and trust that he will do some growing through experience and the discussions.

7. Don't discuss any person who is not present.

It is not fair to teacher, student, parent, etc. if they are not in a position to defend themselves or express their opinions.

8. Don't argue about school policy.

If you are a student, there are things about the system that you cannot change. It is futile to suggest that you do not come to school or quit halfway through the day. The teachers have a responsibility to the principal, the board of education and society — and that is to teach; and you have a responsibility to learn. How you learn is open to discussion. Within the framework of curriculum, marks and expectations are various approaches that teachers and students can discuss together. Topics such as how much input, discovery approach, project method, student presentation and individual or small group research can be presented and considered in group discussions.

The more senior the class, the more likely it is that they can effect changes, but young children who are learning basic skills have less opportunity to change things. But they can express their ideas as persons, and discuss ways of feeling right about themselves, and in their relationships in the class and also within their family.

As a teacher of a junior class of seven to twelve year olds, I use a highly structured approach in the half hour discussion period. From experience I have learned that the discussion is more productive if the school bell ends the session. So we work together from 11:30 to 12:00 noon on a Friday. It could be any day of the week, before recess or at the end of the day; but when the students know that thirty minutes is the maximum, they work harder and proceed more rapidly.

To begin, I write on the blackboard or projectual the following five headings:

1. Good things that occurred in the past week
2. Ways in which we can improve next week
3. Personal problems
4. Responsibilities (monitors)
5. Plans for the future

Working with children under the age of ten I find it better if I act as chairman. Students over the age of ten can rotate the chairmanship, but the teacher should still be the group leader.

The group leader guides the discussion in accordance with the guidelines and maintains order and respect for the rules. Other positions of responsibility can be filled by appointment or election. some of the jobs are agenda collector, secretary, reporter, producer of summary, audio-visual techchnician, treasurer (if money is involved), and recorder of minutes on overhead projectuals, charts, or duplicated copies. It is important that every student have available the summary for the next week. Then he is more likely to participate in group decisions.

These decisions will certainly involve logical consequences for misbehaviour and action plans for future development— and these can always be re-negotiated at the next weekly meeting.

Here are some comments from children in grades Three and Four concerning their classroom discussion periods:
- It's nice to share our problems.
- It's a good feeling to be understood and helped.
- It's nice to be able to help others.
- Thirty heads are better than one.
- We feel more confident now.
- We like to know what to expect in the next week.

- We have learned how to solve our own problems.
- We like to plan extra activities. (creativity)
- It's fun to know how we are all trying to improve in the next week.

Chart 4

Discussion guide for large group (10 or more) which helps to promote democratic principles

Good things in the past week	Ways in which we can improve next week	Problems	Responsibilities	Future plans
Strengths	Decision-making	Problems are the group leader's concern but responsibility for solving problems lies with the group	Jobs to be done in the classroom to be shared and rotated.	Build on positives "What can we do to make our class (group, etc.) more pleasant."
encouragement rather than straight praise	Participation Confrontation		Help to promote cooperation and team spirit	May include plans for fun activities
treat improvement as *group* improvement rather than singling out individuals	Consensus (raise hands)	"What can we do about it" Use a suggestion box		Again responsibility for plans, etc. lies with the group —group will decide if plans are realistic or not.
look for what I can do rather than what you should do				
Discussion period	**Important points**	**Democratic rules**		**Creative tasks or tasks for mischief makers**
30 minutes duration 6 minutes to each topic Leader is chairman first time, then rotate.	Don't waste air time — remember, others want a turn. Contracts to be kept for one week. Emergency meetings only in dire emergencies.	1 Raise your hand. 2 One person speaks at a time. 3 Be responsible. 4 Mutual respect. 5 Be positive. 6 Don't clam up. 7 State your opinion clearly.		Chairman of the week Timer Recorder Committee Chairman

©*by Pearl Cassel and Ruth Gaal 1978*

9
Parent Education— When and by Whom?

How many of us were trained to become parents?

In actuality, the biological equipment is all that is necessary to find ourselves in the most important profession in the world—that of raising the future generations and the perpetuation of our values, skills, and traditions; at the same time, we have to be loving, accepting decision-makers.

Are we qualified to exercise the function of being parents? How many of us received specific training in parenting skills? And how many of us are now finding the task of being a mother or father difficult and frustrating?

How does parent education benefit the public school teacher? I believe that many of our classroom problems would disappear overnight if our pupils' parents were better informed. Discipline and communication would be easier, and many of our job frustrations would change into joys. Every parent must teach the child the meaning of the word *no* from infancy. The child should learn to respect order. This must be done consistently using love and firmness. The growing child must be cultured into a civilized existence in which specific behaviours and rituals are taught methodically. In order to mediate this learning the parent must invest time and patience. Special outings must be planned to provide enjoyment for all. Parenting is an important job involving sacrifice and dedication.

The child, as early as age five, should be taught the tasks, joys and responsibilities of eventually becoming a parent. For example, learning to understand the social structure of families can be taught through stories of puppies, kittens, guppies, etc. Children like to learn how to nurture the young. Have you noticed the excited faces of children watching a mother cat nursing her kittens, or concerned first graders peering into a fish tank and hoping that the baby guppies will survive?

I am very happy to see family-life education for the adolescent becoming part of the curriculum in many schools.

The sexually mature adolescent needs to know the difficult task of being a responsible parent. Some sixteen-year-old girls think that babies are cuddly and cute, but don't realize that in a short time they become demanding toddlers who need much understanding, supervision, and guidance. Some boys think they can claim masculinity by siring a child, yet know nothing about the nurturing process. Some believe that with good luck they can avoid the whole pregnancy process and blindly indulge in the joys of sex.

The following brochures can be obtained from your local Adlerian group:

Co-operation Can be Encouraged
How to be a Good Parent
What's a Family
The A B C's of Guiding the Child
Winning Children Over
The Family Council
The Three R's of Parenting Are—
   Respect, Reason and Responsibility

Children need parents who are strong in their beliefs, values, and self-awareness. They also need to learn self-discipline and limits through understanding the natural or logical consequences of their actions. Children also need the opportunity to participate in decision-making through weekly family council meetings.

The factors that produce a happy family are love, laughter, liberty (within limits), loyalty and learning together.

How these factors are introduced into the family relationship is demonstrated in Adlerian Family Education Centres.

Developing Responsibility

Watch for your child's first attempts to help you or to do things for himself. Encourage these attempts.

Give a child credit for trying to be helpful.

Don't criticize or condemn poor results. Gradually and tactfully steer toward more constructive efforts.

Know when a child is ready for greater responsibilities and then let him take them on.

Let young people know that you trust and have confidence in them.

Always try to set a task that you think the child has a reasonable chance of achieving.

The Well-Adjusted Child—

1. has a feeling of belonging.

2. has a true sense of his own worth.

3. has socially acceptable goals.

4. can meet the needs of a situation.

5. thinks in terms of "we" rather than "I."

6. assumes responsibility.

7. is interested in others.

8. respects the rights of others.

9. is tolerant of others.

10. co-operates with others—adults and peer groups.

11. can work or play happily in a group as well as independently.

Discipline Suggestions for Parents

1. Establish a few clear and consistent methods of discipline when rules are broken.

2. Don't change the rules even if they don't seem to work very well at first. Be consistent and try again.

3. Be simple and direct in talking to your child. Do not question him at length, and avoid long, involved explanations.

4. Parents must present a consistent response to behaviour. Good behaviour is rewarded by a compliment. Poor behaviour is followed by a consequence.

5. The child must realize that he is responsible for his own behaviour, good or bad.

6. Keep the home as calm and quiet as possible. Avoid emotional outbursts in front of your child. Be firm but calm when disciplining.

7. Make shared activities active. Don't expect him to sit still or pay attention for a longer period of time than what is reasonable for his age.

8. Get other children in the family to co-operate with you. Avoid teasing, arguing, fighting, etc., with or in front of the child.

9. Homework should be done in short, quiet work periods, with breaks in between. Set a time limit before he starts, and tell him when the period is over. If he can tell time encourage him to set and monitor his own time schedules.

10. Don't worry about day-to-day fluctuations in control. They are not unusual, and they will gradually decrease as the child becomes more mature.

Creating Positive Self-Concepts

1. Give the child every opportunity to experience *responsibility*—it will help him to become a responsible citizen.

2. Every child needs an opportunity to *contribute*—he will learn to be a contributing member of society.

3. Give the child *freedom of expression* of his ideas and opinions—it will give him a sense of importance and worth.

4. Help him to become a *co-operative* member through sharing activities—he will gain a sense of self-enhancement and personal worth for his contributions to the group.

5. Help him to *appreciate* the attitudes, achievements and ambitions of others.

6. Give ample opportunity for *success*—success builds upon itself. It will help him to build upon productive achievement.

7. Help the child to discover his *talents* and areas of *strength* and to understand his weaknesses and inadequacies—he will learn how to deal successfully with them.

8. *Challenge without threat* stimulates and encourages exploration.

9. *Negate* feelings of *fear*, for they only lead to failure.

10. Provide opportunites for the child to learn to *like himself*—it will give him a sense of dignity.

11. *Listen to the child's message no matter how trivial it may seem—it is a prime technique for showing the child that he is worthy, and it builds confidence in the self.*

12. Don't be afraid to show the child that you *care*—tender love and care will never hurt a healthy relationship—it will be reciprocated throughout the child's life.

10
Understanding the Four Goals

Aggressiveness

Does aggression occur only in relationship to others? If someone punches his fist through a door, does he display aggressive behaviour or merely vent anger and frustration? He may be annoyed with the door because it won't open, or he may be thinking about someone else and acting out hostile feelings. Before we discuss the aggressive child today, the distinction between venting anger and attacking a person or persons must be considered. I think it would be best if we came to a common understanding of the word *aggressive*.

There are many different views of what aggression is. According to the Oxford distionary, aggression is an unprovoked attack, the first attack in a quarrel, an assault; and to be aggressive is to be offensive. Perhaps we usually think of an aggressive child in these terms, but the derivation of the word is from the Latin *aggressare*, meaning "to approach."

Many people are confused by the terms *aggressive* and *assertive*. *Assertion* is the act of protecting one's own property. *Aggression* is the act of attacking someone else or forcibly attempting to claim another person's property.

Adlerian psychologists believe that all behaviour is purposive and goal-directed toward feelings of belonging and having a place in a social group. Young children, by trial and error, *approach* their mother, father, siblings and classmates and learn from the reactions of others. If these interpersonal relationships are healthy, loving, encouraging and involved with setting reasonable limits, the child will grow with good feelings about himself, and feel that he has a valuable place in his family or school. On the other hand, if a child is discouraged in his attempts to approach others in a positive way, he will likely change his approach to being negative, hostile, or aggressive, because due to his own private faulty logic, he figures that the only way to count is to be noticed, and that it is better to get nagging or punishing attention from adults than no attention at all.

Testing, Testing

Since the young child is continually testing his ability to communicate with others, and he depends on adult reaction for his status, he may conclude one or more of the following:
- I only count when I am the boss.
- I only count when people pay special attention to me.
- If people don't let me do what I want, they don't love me.
- I must hurt people before they get a chance to hurt me because all people are mean.
- The only way to make them understand what I want is by bullying them.

These faulty conclusions are apperceptions—his interpretation of how things are from his eyes, ears, and shoes, and not necessarily actual fact. And if he interprets (sees) the world this way, his behaviour will most likely be hostile, pushy and aggressive.

However, when we deal with aggressive children it is most important that we first check for other possible causes, such as health problems, toothache, earache, insufficient sleep, language difficulty, hearing impairment, visual or auditory perception, inappropriate diet, etc; or problems—a domineering father, mother or teacher; or frustration about not being able to reach goals set by others at home or school. A favored sibling may cause a less attractive child to feel neglected and hated. All behaviour is movement toward or away from others. This moving approach may be co-operative and contributing, or hostile and aggressive. *All* movement is *purposive.*

Alfred Adler early in his career, unlike Freud, felt that the motive of aggression was more important than sexuality. Later he called aggression a "will-to-power," and finally, at the end of his life, stated that the striving for superiority—a striving to overcome inferiority and inadequacy—was the main universal goal in life. This is analogous to Jung's concept of self (introvert and extrovert) or Goldstein's principle of self-actualization (to become competent), supported by Maslow and other Humanists. All children have feelings of inferiority. Normal children strive to overcome these feelings by striving for goals primarily social in character. The neurotic or maladjusted child strives for power and self-aggrandizement. The child who needs particular guidance and training is one in whom abnormal manifestations occur because of exaggerated feelings of either superiority or inferiority.

Presently, many parents who model their behaviour on the traditional autocratic family of the past—in which the authoritarian father was the boss, and the mother and children were subservient to his demands—are now experiencing great difficulties in raising their children.

Now that our society is politically democratic the power of authorities is continually being challenged. Women and children have for several years been questioning the absolute power of the husband-father and feeling that they are also entitled to participate in decision-making. This struggle for power corrupts and destroys the harmony in many homes because our society has not trained individuals in how to live democratically.

One of the key techniques for helping members of a family to understand each other better is by discussing and analysing with each other the life-style of the mother, father, and each child (see Chapter 1). When the pattern of life goals is disclosed, deeper understanding and communications skills can be learned. The analysis involves asking the individual about his family constellation and early recollections. The answers help the therapist to form a clear picture of the personality development and life goals of the subject. This life-style is firmly developed before age eight and cannot be changed without therapy.

The style of life determines the unique individuality of each person. Each child creates his own life-style from his hereditary abilities and his environmental impressions. A life-style has many components. An important contributing factor is the family constellation. The individuals most responsible for helping a child develop a life-style are not only the parents, but also the siblings who are most different. A boy who is a middle child between two girls may develop an aggressive life-style committed to provoking because he feels unable to compete favorably with the quiet co-operative girls. Let us consider some generalities about how the family constellation affects the life-styles of the children.

In families that function as a co-operative unit, where mutual respect is modelled by the parents and actively taught to the children by democratic training, there are very few children displaying undue aggression. Conversely, where families are highly competitive, where the three P's—power, prestige and profit—are priority family values, most family members will be aggressive, even a family with only one child. In families where there is less competition, there are usually fewer differences in the personalities of the children.

Democratic families work and play together. They listen to each other. They respect each other. They have family council meetings. They are friends.

We can speculate on how it happens that a family may have just one aggressive child. We have all heard parents say, "My children are all easy to get along with except one fellow. Our boy Jack is always in trouble. We can't understand how the others are all so good, and he is so bad."

The Family Constellation

Most commonly the aggressive child is the middle child of three. He may be uncertain of his place since he has neither the rights of the oldest nor the privileges of the youngest.

From this situation he may feel that people are unfair to him. If the oldest is capable and the youngest is attractive, he may become a "problem" if he feels discouraged. He may feel squeezed out, and in retaliation may feel an obligation to squeeze others. He may also feel neglected and unloved.

Similarly, in a large family, the second child may be opposite to the first child, who is "good," so he may act as if he were in a race and may overcompensate and become hyperactive and pushy.

A first child who has been the only child and center of interest and attention becomes dethroned by a new baby. He may feel, "They don't love me anymore." After dethronement, he may seek undue attention on the destructive side and become a problem child. He is often overly concerned with his own prestige and feels he has to be first. And if he can't be first best, he will settle for being first worst.

The youngest child is often spoiled by parents and older siblings. He may become "boss" of the whole family and feel entitled to have his own way.

The only boy among girls may feel unsure of his place, but more often he becomes the "little prince" and eventually his view of life is "I am king of the world and all of you people have to do as I say."

The only girl among boys may become the little princess, a tomboy, or feel isolated. If she feels alienation, she may overcompensate by feeling a compulsion to be pushy and bossy.

A child born after the death of a sibling is often overprotected by over-anxious parents. The deceased may be unrealistically idealized. One cannot compete with a ghost and so one is frustrated to the point of hostility and aggression. Presently at our school we are dealing with a very hostile six-year-old boy whose ten-year-old brother has terminal cancer. The mother naturally is very distressed, and spoiling both children to the point where the six-year-old feels entitled to do anything he likes without concern for others.

An only child who has associated mostly with adults may feel lonesome and resent not having siblings. He is frequently interested only in himself and considers every situation in terms of "What's in it for me?" He is often a "getter" rather than a "doer." If requests are not granted, he may feel unfairly treated, refuse to co-operate and become hostile.

There are varying degrees of aggressivesness, ranging from the acceptable active, creative, inventive youngster to the hyperactive, selfish, malicious disturber who may physically attack others. Analysing the family constellation is the prime clue to finding a possible explanation for the child's behaviour.

Faulty Logic

The first course of action is preventing children from developing faulty logic about how to find their place in the family or social group. I suggest a strenuous parent education program. If parents learn how to raise children democratically instead of competitively, they are less likely to produce overly aggressive children. The next course is to teach parents and teachers how to handle hostile children by not falling for the child's provocation and reinforcing his faulty logic; and by withdrawing from conflict, and modelling friendly behaviour with firmness and kindness. Finally and maybe the most important course is for us to learn how to be encouraging, because discouraged children always become behaviour problems.

Although the long-range goals of the life-style are difficult to change, the immediate goals of aggressive behaviour can be dealt with quite simply; and with children under ten there are only four goals. When the behaviour is modified and the child feels encouraged and more confident about his place and sense of worth, his motivation may change and he may in turn change his own life-style. So, with aggressive children, the beginning of change consists of modifying the motivation of immediate behaviour.

A misbehaving child is always a discouraged child. He desperately wants to "belong," so he acts on the faulty logic that his misbehaviour will give him the social acceptance he desires.

If we can first understand the four goals of the child's misbehaviour and then practice effective methods of correction, we are in a position to correct both the behaviour and the mistaken goal. Modifying just the behaviour is not enough; we must also modify the motivation. This may be done much more easily with young children and is particularly effective with pre-school children.

In our culture, young children have few opportunities to make useful contributions toward the welfare of the group. Adults, or older siblings, do whatever needs to be done, and the young child finds few ways to help. It is easier for a child growing up on a farm, where there are many necessary chores to be performed, to feel that his part of the work is a necessary and vital contribution. In our more affluent and urban way of life, many children make no real contribution. Even those who do have chores often become easily discouraged when they compare their inept performance with the more efficient accomplishments of adults or older siblings.

"I Want Attention"

When the child is deprived of the opportunity to gain status through useful contributions, he usually seeks proof of his acceptance in his family through getting attention. He has the "faulty logic" that only if people pay attention to him does he have a place in the world. But getting attention is not a way of developing his self-confidence, nor does it develop his self-reliance. So he develops an insatiable appetite for attention, and requires ever-increasing amounts of it in a misguided attempt to "belong."

Usually he first tries to find his place through pleasant and socially acceptable means. He may make cute remarks or do stunts. Often he gives the impression of excellence, and this is a source of delight to many parents and teachers. Why, then, is it called "misbehaviour"? Because his goal is not to learn or to co-operate, but rather to elevate himself to gain special attention. The maladjustment becomes apparent when praise and recognition are not forthcoming. The the "good" performance stops (see Chart 5, page 91). If the child is the "passive" type, his methods for getting attention are of a passive nature. These children, too, are "model" children and are often "teacher's pet."

As mentioned before, demands for attention keep increasing, and sooner or later many of these children are no longer satisfied with the amounts of attention they receive by using socially acceptable means; and as they become discouraged, they switch to the "useless side." They become destructive attention-seekers. This includes the "show-off" who becomes somewhat obnoxious, the "clown" who tends to bother us, the mischief-maker, the "brat" who makes a nuisance of himself, and the child who keeps us occupied with him.

If the "charm" type becomes discouraged in his first methods of passively keeping us busy, he, too, usually switches to the useless side, and becomes destructive in a passive way. We type him as "lazy," as long as his goal is to get extra attention and service. These children manage to put others in their service by being "inept." They require adults to "help" them and, since children usually manage adults much better than adults manage children, we adults usually fall for their manipulations. So we remind, coax, pick up after them, reassure them whenever they show fear, and act in a way which only further reaffirms their faulty evaluation of their lack of ability.

For a child who is seeking attention as his goal in life, being ignored is intolerable. He will accept punishment, pain, humiliation, etc., in order to get extra attention or service. An adult who allows himself to be kept busy, who gives the child extra service, who nags, coaxes, reminds and constantly advises—feels annoyed at the child. Even if the child is using socially acceptable means of attention-getting, the adult has the feeling that he is being kept unduly busy. Thus, in behaving in the "natural" way, the adult only fortifies the misbehaving child's faulty logic and encourages his mistaken goal.

What should he do? He may give the child lots of attention at other times, but not when he is seeking it. He should recognize that an attention-seeking child, even one who is using constructive methods, is a somewhat discouraged child. The treatment for all misbehaviour is to encourage (not just to praise) the child. Help the child who is using destructive methods to use constructive methods; and then further encourage him to find his place without seeking attention, but rather, by making useful contributions to the group. In other words, help the child develop his "social interest" and thus become well-adjusted.

"I'm The Boss"

But what of the child who has become still further discouraged? If he has not attained his mistaken goal of getting attention and has not been encouraged to find healthy methods of increasing his self-esteem, he usually finds the attention is not enough. Then he changes his goal to that of power (Goal Two). The power-seeking child operates on the faulty logic, "If you don't let me do what I want, you don't love me" or

"I only count when you do what I want you to do." In many ways the goal of power is similar to that of destructive attention-getting, but it is more intense and words are used as weapons.

The active type often argues, contradicts, lies, may have violent temper tantrums, refuse to do what he is told to do, continues forbidden acts, and may refuse to do his work, or little of it, and is openly disobedient. If he is of the passive type, his laziness is much more pronounced so that he usually does no work at all, or he "forgets," becomes stubborn, and is passively disobedient.

The adult's reaction to a power-seeking child is to feel that his leadership is threatened. He thinks, "Who is controlling this situation? He or I? He vows, He can't get away with this! I won't let him do this to me!" But these efforts to control or force a power-drunk child are usually futile. The child will win about 99% of the time; and if the adult succeeds in overcoming him and defeating him he usually becomes even more rebellious, and may then seek revenge. If the adult wins the struggle today, the child will usually win tomorrow. No final "victory" is possible. And the longer the power struggle continues, the more the child becomes convinced that power has value; thus, his mistaken goal is reinforced. His "faulty logic" seems strange to adults, but it makes sense to him. He still wants to "belong," although his methods of finding his place do not have the effect of winning friends—and many of these children desperately want friends. They try to force others to play with them, and then get disappointed or angry when other children don't do what they want.

What can the adult do to help him correct his mistaken convictions? He may teach the child how to share not just toys, but choices and time itself. He may as well admit that the child has as much power as he has. If he fights with him, the child will win. So he should avoid getting into a power-struggle with him and extricate himself from the conflict. He might as well recognize the child's power.

The pupil expects the teacher will fight with him and he may well relish the prospect of the struggle. We tell parents that an effective way of extricating themselves from a power struggle is to go to the bathroom. Is this defeat? No, because the parent is simply refusing to fight with the child. In the classroom, a way to deal with the situation would be to recognize that the power-seeking child is always ambitious, and try to redirect his ambition to useful channels. He might be enlisted to help another child, or be given a position of responsibility that he feels has some prestige. Rather than threatening him, as he anticipates, the teacher may appeal to him for help, even saying "I cannot make you do it and I know I can't." This may disarm him and enlist his cooperation. An appeal to him for advice and assistance will be more effective than threats. If the adult acknowledges the child's superiority in his ability to defeat him, he "takes his sail out of the child's wind" and there is no longer any use in his "blowing." Power is only important when it is contested. Actually, we should respect a power-seeking child for the ability he has to upset authorities. Any child who has his parents, the teacher, the helping teacher, principal, school psychologist and nurse all upset, deserves a certain amount of credit!

"I'll Get You for This"

If, however, the desire for power no longer suffices, or the child feels so beaten down that he no longer seeks to win the power struggle but seeks to retaliate, he uses Goal Three—revenge. The revenge-seeking child is so deeply discouraged that he feels that only by hurting others can he find his place, since others seem to always hurt him. Convinced that he is hopelessly disliked, he will respond with deep distrust to the adult's efforts to convince him otherwise. And, since his goal is to hurt others as he feels hurt by them, he is seemingly "unlovable." His actions are vicious, violent and brutal. He is openly defiant and is a potential delinquent, if not already one. He knows the vulnerability of others, whom he sees as "opponents," and he is out to hurt them. He considers it a victory when he is labelled as vicious, since this seems to be the only triumph open to him. He may injure his classmates, animals, adults, and he may scratch, bite and kick. He is a sore loser and immediately starts plotting revenge for his defeat, usually by even more violent methods than those used before. Leaders of juvenile delinquent gangs are usually Goal Three-behaving children who see the whole of society as their enemy, and frequently look down on others with contempt.

Yet underneath the facade, they are deeply discouraged individuals with little hope for themselves. Usually they are active, but occasionally we find one who is sullen and defiant in a "violent passivity," and this type is even more deeply discouraged.

Revenge-seeking children are very difficult to deal with, and may require professional help. Punishment will only produce more rebellion, so it is to be avoided. Natural consequences may be applied. But the main goal of the adult should be to try to win and persuade the child that he can be liked. This is difficult because much of his behaviour will deny that this is possible. The class or family as a group may be enlisted to help, but the adult must take steps to assure that the group will not make things worse by turning against the discouraged child. "Good" children often enlist themselves in an alliance with the adult against the "bad" children, and this must be avoided. But group discussions may help to promote mutual understanding and help. Sometimes the adult may enlist the help of one child who may have some empathy with the discouraged child, and may be willing to be a "buddy" to him. It should be remembered that if a revenge-seeking child becomes power-seeking only, that is progress. And if he only seeks undue attention and service, that is further progress in his rehabilitation. The most important thing in dealing with a revenge-seeking child who is out to hurt the adult is for the adult not to become hurt by him.

"I Want to Be Alone!"

A passive child or one whose antagonism is successfully beaten down may become so deeply discouraged that he gives up all hope of significance, and expects only failure and defeat. He may actually feel hopeless, or he may assume this position in order to avoid any further opportunities that might be embarrassing or humiliating to him. Thus he uses his "inability" as a protective shield (inferiority complex). His actions appear "stupid" and he rarely participates; and by his extreme ineptitude he prevents anything being demanded or expected of him. Many children who appear to be dull are quite capable but are so deeply discouraged that they convince us that they are "hopeless." Some of these may be brilliant children but use Goal Four in a mistaken attempt to cope with a world which they view as extremely discouraging.

It is very difficult for an adult not to fall for the child's provocation that "you can't do anything with me, so leave me alone." The natural reaction is for the adult to give up. The child's discouragement is contagious, but it is important that the teacher or parent not yield to this provocation as much as he is inclined to do so. Great amounts of encouragement are needed, and the child must be encouraged even when he makes mistakes. Every possible attempt should be made to help the discouraged child feel worthwhile. The adult may best help by a sincere conviction that there is hope for the child and that he will not give up with him.

The most frequent deteriorating sequences that result from deepening discouragement on the child's part are—

- active-constructive attention-getting, to
- active-destructive attention-getting, to
- active-destructive power, to
- active-destructive revenge.

or

- passive-constructive attention-getting, to
- passive-destructive attention-getting, to
- display of inadequacy.

or

- passive-constructive attention-getting, to
- display of inadequacy.

Recognition and Confrontation

Adults may soon become quite skillful in understanding the goals of children by observing them. The younger the child the easier it is to recognize his goal in any given situation. Older children are less obvious, and by the time a child reaches adolescence he has learned to disguise his behaviour so that the goals are not obvious. Probably the most accurate clue to discovering the young child's goal is to observe your instinctive response to his behaviour. Your instinctive response is usually in line with the child's expectations.

Thus:

- if adult feels annoyed—indicates Goal One—attention-getting;

- if adult feels defeated or threatened — Goal Two — power;
- if adult feels deeply hurt — Goal Three — revenge;
- if adult feels helpless — Goal Four — display of inadequacy.

Another indication of the goal is to observe the child's response to correction. If the child is seeking attention and gets it from the adult, he will stop the misbehaviour temporarily, and then probably repeat it before long. If he seeks power, he will refuse to stop the disturbance or he may even increase it. If he seeks revenge, his response to the adult's efforts to get him to stop will be to switch to some more violent action. A Goal Four child will not co-operate but will remain entirely passive and inactive.

Confrontation is another method that can be used but must be done properly, and should not imply criticism or be humiliating to the child. The atmosphere must be friendly and the disclosure must not be made at the time of conflict. The emphasis is not on "why," but on "for what purpose." "Why" implies emphasis on the past, whereas "for what purpose" implies his present intentions. Nothing can be done about the past, so a discussion about that is pointless and may also be inaccurate. However, the purpose in the child's present behaviour can be determined and his intentions may be changed. An accurate questioning regarding the child's present intentions produces a "recognition reflex," and the facial expression is an accurate indication of his goal even though the child may say nothing or even say No. The recognition reflex is often a roguish smile or a twinkle of the eyes or even a twitch of a facial muscle. Sometimes it is so open that the child covers his face or bursts into laughter. The child should always be asked whether he would like to know the purpose of his behaviour. Usually he is quite willing. The adult should offer the interpretation in an indirect way: "I wonder if...", "Could it be that...", "I have a feeling that...". If there is no reaction, no recognition reflex, the adult may make another guess.

Suggested questions:

Goal One: "Could it be that you want me to pay attention to you?" "... keep me busy with you."

Goal Two: "Could it be that you want to be the boss?" "... to show me that you can do what you want to do and that no one can stop you."

Goal Three: "Could it be that you want to hurt me and the children in the class?" "... you want to get even?"

Goal Four: "Could it be that you want to be left alone?" "... you think you are stupid and you don't want anyone to find out?"

When the recognition reflex occurs, the corrective procedures must immediately follow. These will be discussed later.

In summary, if we want to help a child we must attempt to see with his eyes, hear with his ears, and stand in his shoes. "It is not what happens to us but how we feel about it that counts." As pointed out before, all the goals of children's misbehaviour are the result of the child's "faulty logic." However, this is how he sees and interprets events. By engaging the child in friendly conversations, by listening to his side of the story, by actually playing with him, the adult may gain insights into ways to help the child to correct his faulty interpretations, and acquire more adequate solutions. Group discussions are also very helpful in correcting the child's faulty evaluations.

Don't fall for his provocations; use logical and natural consequences rather than reward and punishment. Practice mutual respect and encourage the child to correct his behaviour, and he will grow into a healthy, contributing adult.

The adult should attempt to −

1. not fall for the child's provocations.

2. use logical consequences instead of reward and punishment.

3. encourage the child.

4. practise mutual respect.

Remember that by training a child we are helping him to grow into a healthy, independent, contributing adult.

Identifying the goals of children's misbehaviour

INCREASED SOCIAL INTEREST ← | → DIMINISHED SOCIAL INTEREST

MINOR DISCOURAGEMENT ← | → DEEP DISCOURAGEMENT

USEFUL AND SOCIALLY ACCEPTABLE BEHAVIOUR		USELESS AND UNACCEPTABLE BEHAVIOUR		GOALS
Active constructive	*Passive constructive*	*Active destructive*	*Passive destructive*	
Success Cute remarks Excellence for praise and recognition Performing for attention Stunts for attention Being especially good Being industrious Being reliable *(May seem to be ideal student, but goal is self-evaluation, not co-operation)*	**Charm** Excess pleasantness Model child Bright sayings Exaggerated conscientiousness Excess charm	**Nuisance** The show off The clown Walking question mark Enfant terrible Instability Acts tough. Makes minor mischief.	**Laziness** Bashfulness Lack of ability Instability Lack of stamina Fearfulness Speech impediments Untidiness Self-indulgence Frivolity Anxiety Eating difficulties Performance difficulties	**GOAL 1** **Attention-getting** Seeks proof of his approval or status (almost universal in pre-school children). Will cease when reprimanded or given attention.
	Respects rights of others. Is tolerant of others. Co-operates with others. Encourages others. Is courageous. Has a true sense of own worth.	**Rebel** Argues Contradicts Continues forbidden acts. Temper tantrums Bad habits Untruthfulness Dawdling	**Stubborn** Disobedience Forgetting	**GOAL 2** **Power** Similar to destructive attention-getting, but more intense. Reprimand intensifies misbehaviour.
The well-adjusted child has most of these qualities	Has a feeling of belonging. Has socially acceptable goals. Willing to share rather than thinking, "How much can I get?" "We" rather than "I."	**Vicious** Stealing Bed-wetting Violent and brutal (leader of juvenile delinquent gangs)	**Violent passivity** Sullen Defiant	**GOAL 3** **Revenge** Does things to hurt others. Makes self hated. Retaliates.
			Hopeless Stupidity (pseudo feeble-minded) Indolence Ineptitude Inferiority complex	**GOAL 4** **Display of inadequacy** Assumes real or imagined deficiency to safeguard prestige.

This chart describes the behaviours of discouraged children up to ten years of age.
Moving from Goals 4 to 3 (and so on) is a sign of improvement in the child's behaviour.

By Pearl Cassel, June 1973 (adapted from chart by Edith Dewey).

How to correct children's misbehaviour®

by Pearl Cassel

Chart 6

BY INTERPRETATION OF THE FOUR MISTAKEN GOALS

UP TO 10 YEARS OLD

Child's action and attitude	Teacher's reaction	Ask these specific questions to diagnose . . .	Corrective procedure
Nuisance Show off Clown Lazy Puts others in his service, keeps teacher busy. Thinks, "He occupies too much of my time." "Only when people pay attention to me do I have a place."	**Feels annoyed.** Gives service. Is kept busy. Reminds often. Coaxes. Thinks, "He occupies too much of my time." "I wish he would not bother me."	**GOAL 1** **Attention** A. "Could it be that you want me to notice you?" OR B. "Could it be that you want me to do something special for you?"	**Never give attention when child demands it.** Ignore the misbehaving child who is bidding for attention. (Punishing, nagging, giving service, advising, is attention.) Do not show annoyance. Be firm. Give lot of attention at any other time.
Stubborn Argues. Wants to be the boss. Temper tantrums Tells lies. Disobedient Does opposite to instructions. Does little or no work. Says, "If you don't let me do what I want you don't love me." Thinks, "I only count if you do what I want."	**Feels defeated.** Teacher's leadership is threatened Thinks, "He can't do this to me." "Who is running the class? He or I?" "He can't get away with this."	**GOAL 2** **Power** A. "Could it be that you want to show me that you can do what you want and no one can stop you?" OR B. "Could it be that you want to be boss?"	**Don't fight—don't give in.** Recognize and admit that the child has power. Give power in situations where child can use power productively. Avoid power struggle. Extricate yourself from the conflict. Take your sails out of his wind. Ask for his aid. Respect child. Make agreement.
Vicious Steals. Sullen Defiant Dislikes child. Will hurt animals, peers and adults. Tries to hurt as he feels hurt by others. Kicks, bites, scratches. Sore loser Potential delinquent Thinks, "My only hope is to get even with them."	**Feels deeply hurt.** Outraged. Dislikes child. Retaliates (continual conflict). Thinks, "How mean can he be?" "How can I get even with him?"	**GOAL 3** **Revenge** A. "Could it be that you want to hurt me and the pupils in the class? OR B. "Could it be that you want to get even?"	**Never say you are hurt.** Don't behave as though you are. Apply natural consequences. (Punishment produces more rebellion.) Do the unexpected. Persuade child that he is liked. Use group encouragement. Enlist one buddy. Try to convince him that he is liked
Feels hopeless "Stupid" actions Inferiority complex Gives up. Tries to be left alone. Rarely participates. Says, "You can't do anything with me." Thinks, "I don't want anyone to know how inadequate I am."	**Feels helpless.** Throws up hands. Doesn't know what to do. Thinks, "I don't know what to do with him." "I give up." "I can't do anything with him."	**GOAL 4** **Display of inadequacy** A. "Could it be that you want to be left alone?" OR B. "Could it be that you feel stupid and don't want people to know?"	**Encourage when he makes mistakes.** Make him feel worthwhile. Praise him when he tries. Say, "I do not give up with you." Avoid support of inferior feelings. Constructive approach. Get class co-operation with pupil helpers. Avoid discouragement yourself.

11
Growth of the Self-Concept in Youth

Today's adolescents are struggling for self-identity and acceptance by their peers. Entwined in their struggles they fear rejection from the group, and they fear their own inadequacies.
They are ashamed of their clumsy bodies and pimply skin.
They are embarrassed and afraid they will never find a sexual
partner. They feel guilty about separating from mother (the
umbilical cord syndrome) and even more guilty about dis-
obeying father.

If teenagers feel so confused, it's no wonder teachers and
parents are even more confused about the way young people
behave or misbehave.

In the past, their struggles for identity were not as pro-
longed because they were dealt with by traditions and cere-
monies. By performing certain cultural rituals the young
people could see and pass certain milestones along the way of
growing into adulthood.

Most cultures were autocratic, with parents, teachers,
church and state being in authority. Parents felt secure and
justified in stating that adult freedoms were the reward for
hard work and dedication to family values, adherence to or-
thodox religious beliefs, and resisting the temptations of sin.

There were many guidelines for acceptable behaviour. Certain tasks had to be performed at specific ages: no shame was
to be brought upon the family name; one behaved as a male

or a female in stereotyped roles. Society continually judged the adolescents for proof, and youth was assured that the prize of adulthood was within grasp.

Here are a few examples of adolescent milestones from the past; few families still hold these requirements of their children:

1. Rigid passing grades at school before entry to a higher level.

2. Confirmation or Bar Mitzvah as recognition for spiritual independence and personal responsibility.

3. Graduation from school at age fourteen.

4. Proof of cooking and sewing ability for a girl to be a prospective wife.

5. Proof of a good job for a prospective husband.

6. Betrothal was the prerequisite for unchaperoned dating.

7. Coming-of-age the prerequisite for free use of the door key for entry and exit.

8. Marriage was the sanction for sexual activity. Usually girls couldn't get married unless the male asked the girl's parents' permission.

9. Financial or property independence was required before a man could set up his own domicile.

10. If a girl got pregnant she was forced to marry.

From anthropological studies we find highly specialized initiation rites, enforced by the chief of the band or tribe.

In some North American Indian tribes the aspiring boy was initiated into the adult community only after he had climbed a mountain, found an eagle's nest, struggled with the fierce eagles, taken a feather, clambered down the mountain and given the feather to his chief—only then was he a man.

That was the past.

Today many of our young people are confused and need counsellors to guide them through the very difficult process of maturing in a democratic society.

And it is even more difficult now because society is changing its attitude every few years. Even though we are politically democratic, democracy is still an unreached ideal. Parents and teachers hold fast to their conditioning, which was probably autocratic. It is the crucial role of counsellors with democratic skills to show the way by helping young people to develop a new self-concept based on mutual respect.

How can we as counsellors, teachers or parents help our young people who are presently depressed or even contemplating suicide?

It seems to me they all want a feeling of belonging and are struggling so desperately to find it. They are trying to find their place in the world, in their classrooms and in or out of their families. Most of their confusions are social in nature. They may present other concerns such as problems with courses, or teachers, or parents, but basically they are saying, "Who am I? What am I? Where am I going? Am I acceptable? Will they like me? Can I make it? How can I develop a positive self-concept when I feel so inadquate?"

Communication problems

Many adolescents struggle frantically for acceptance by the opposite sex. When finally they connect, find a mate (even for five minutes) they get a burning desire to say, "Hey mum, I can do it! I have made it through this torture of desire and the unknown. I wanted so much to prove that I am capable and can make it sexually." But due to religious, cultural, and societal norms that have conditioned the conscience, as well as the taboos that have imposed restrictions, jubilation is impossible. So they resort to guilt feelings and deviousness and various methods of blocking communication in order that they never express their real feelings of arrival at manhood or womanhood. So the battle of silence and mixed messages prevails between parents and adolescents in this "liberated" society.

It was okay to say, "Mum, look at me" when at age five he learned how to skate, but his entering the adult world is threatening to many parents, and so is left unsaid.

In order to help a teenager develop a feeling of worth we must build on strengths. What are his assets? As the counsellor, teacher or parent you can help by asking the teenager to write a list of his strengths and together with him find out where he needs to do some more learning. Because the old milestones are not here anymore, you set goals together with him as objectives and commitments. He must see what he already has to offer society, what he needs to learn, and how he can fit into the system that offers opportunity for all. Your job is to help the teenager to feel okay about himself so he can cope with interpersonal relating skills.

There are various interpretations for growth or self-concept. We have been exposed to the following schools of thought. Carl Rogers taught us how to relate; William Glasser stresses that we avoid giving a student a failing identity; Dr. Frederick Perls taught us how to use Gestalt therapy, and we have all learned how to use ourselves in the communication process. Thomas Gordon has given us skills especially in active listening; and transactional analysis has provided a workable model of specific techniques. We have become eclectic through our learning and experience.

Self-concept

How did we develop our own positive self-concepts? We were probably accepted, loved, nurtured and encouraged by our parents. We had satisfying relationships with our siblings. At school we likely achieved well and grew with a sense of accomplishment. During adolescence we enjoyed the group feeling of being with non-judgmental friends. Our plans for the future involved aiming for one chosen career because the job market was open. Our country needed workers in those days and we knew that we could get a job, earn our money, contribute to the community and have a sense of worth.

Today the teenagers that we talk with are on more shaky ground. Many of them do not have such firm foundations or predictable futures. They may have as many as five careers in their lifetime, or none at all.

If our self-concepts (I am this, that and the other) are similar to our self-ideals (I should or must be this, that or the other) — we are well balanced and can maintain a sane equilibrium. On the other hand, if our self-concepts are very different from our self-ideals we become torn with inner conflicts and frustrations due to the struggles within us. These struggles sap our nervous energy and diminish our potential for problem solving, effective decision-making and healthy interpersonal coping skills.

We enter the Intrapsychic Cycle of Discouragement (see Chart 8), and resort to Negative Nonsense. If we are into Negative Nonsense we start laying blame to relieve our own guilt feelings.

We blame ourselves and get depressed, or we blame others and become paranoiac or we blame life and try to escape. If we function with blaming, we search for proof as evidence. So we become very critical of ourselves or others and then become miserable. Within our misery we may become aggressive or violent or addicted to alcohol or drugs—or even suicidal.

Young people may exhibit any or all three of these symptoms of discouragement to us. What can we do to help?

I suggest that we do a life-style analysis, which involves dealing with all five components, i.e., self-concept, self ideals, view of the world, assets, and self-defeating mechanisms (see Chapter 1). We would use the family constellation, parents' expectations, sexual development, early recollections and recurrent dreams as diagnostic tools. The life-style will emerge as one of the following typologies (described in Chapter 4):

1. The Controller
2. The Driver
3. The person who needs to be Right
4. The person who needs to be Good
5. The person who needs to be Liked
6. The person who needs to be Superior
7. The Getter
8. The Aginner
9. The person who Avoids Feelings
10. The person who feels Inadequate
11. The Excitement-Seeker

12. The Martyr

13. The Victim

14. The Baby

The Courage to Be Imperfect

If you have no time to do full analysis, just have the client list his strengths and then state his "shoulds." Concentrate on the strengths and build with encouragement. Teach the client to have the "courage to be imperfect."

Many teenagers are overambitious and feel that they will never make it. They are frightened by their feelings of inadequacy. They want to be 100% all the time.

Teach them that 70% is okay and normal. Give them permission to try things and make mistakes, otherwise they will not try at all. Encourage them to take one step at a time. Ask them what they are willing to do as a start, then sign a contract of commitment with them. After one week evaluate the progress together and make a new contract.

Group counselling, using values-education exercises and values-clarification games can be helpful to teenagers with low self-esteem.

When we can understand our own motivations we become more able to empathize with others and see what makes them tick. Then we can communicate more effectively and increase our sense of belonging and self-concept. As we share our thoughts and feelings with others we become more aware of our similarities and connectedness. Respecting differences is important to rid our society of prejudice, but realizing how similar we all are helps us to really love our fellow man.

The Four Priorities

Wilmer Pew, a famous Adlerian, used a technique for helping counsellors to understand themselves and to help their clients. It is based on the work of Nera Kfir.

He discovered that basically people are in one of four categories. Our priority motivation is one of the following:

1. To please

2. To control

3. To seek personal comfort

4. To be significant or superior.

How do you find out which is your priority situation? What we try to avoid most is the major clue.

If we try to avoid rejection we are probably Pleasers.

If we try to avoid humiliation we are probably Controllers.

If we try to avoid tension we are probably Comfort-Seekers.

If we try to avoid meaninglessness we probably like to feel Superior.

All interpersonal relating skills are based on reciprocal exchange. This means that within ourselves there is a marketplace, and we alone decide the price that we are willing to pay.

Pleasers pay the price of reduced personal growth.

Controllers pay the price of loss of spontaneity and loss of friends.

Comfort-Seekers pay the price of reduced productivity.

Superiors pay the price of feeling continually over-burdened.

How do we, both counsellors and students, cope in conflict situations?

What are our interpersonal relationship skills? I suggest the possible outcomes of conflict are as follows:

If we are Pleasers the opponent probably feels pleased with the present outcome, but lacks respect, if this strategy is used repeatedly ad nauseum.

If we are Controllers the opponent probably feels considerable tension.

If we are Comfort-Seekers the opponent probably feels irritation and a sense of "unfinished business."

If Superiority is our goal then other people feel inadequate when we confront them.

If young people can develop a positive self-concept they will be able to cope with the problems of life, make appropriate decisions from a selection of alternatives, and deal with criticism or conflict in positive and constructive ways.

I suggest the following procedures for solving conflict situations and saving face, and at the same time promoting self-esteem and enhancing self-concept.

Ten Commandments for Resolving Conflict

1. Don't lose your temper; you'll lose your point.

2. Remember, you are trying to reach an agreement, not win an argument.

3. Apologize when you're wrong, even on a minor matter.

4. Don't imply superior knowledge or power.

5. Acknowledge with grace the significance of the other's comment or statement or fact.

6. Know and admit the impact of your demands.

7. Remember that the ability to separate fact from opinion is the mark of a clear mind and reflects intellectual integrity.

8. Stay with your point; pursue your objective but don't devastate.

9. Don't quibble; say what you mean and mean what you say. If you want truth, give it.

10. Bargain in good faith. Your intellect will tell you when you're bargaining and your conscience will tell you whether you have good faith.

We are all in the growth process of becoming self-actualized. Our teenagers are in their particular place along the continuum. We can help them to appreciate their assets and continue their growth. Self-concept is personal, and dependent on skills and experience. We can encourage them to take responsibility for their own behaviour, accept their own mistakes and learn from them, to step forward into adulthood with confidence and a positive self-concept that says, "This is what I am, these are my skills. I want to contribute, I want to improve. Please accept me as I am, but teach me how to grow some more."

Chart 7

Personality priorities

PRIORITY	PRICE PAID	TRIES TO AVOID MOST	OTHER PEOPLE'S REACTION
1 *Comfort*	Reduced Productivity	Stress	Irritation
2 *Pleasing*	Reduced Growth	rejection	Pleased
3 *Control*	Reduced Spontaneity	Humiliation	Tension
4 *Superiority*	Feels Overburdened	Meaningless-ness	Feel Inadequate

Chart 7A

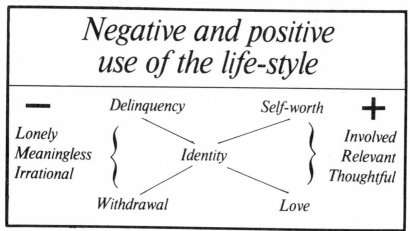

Negative and positive use of the life-style

Adapted from William Glasser

Chart 8

Intrapsychic cycle of discouragement

An encouraged person has:—
- High self-esteem/self concept.
- Self-identity/feelings of worth.
- Social interest—feelings of belonging and connectedness, similarity to others.

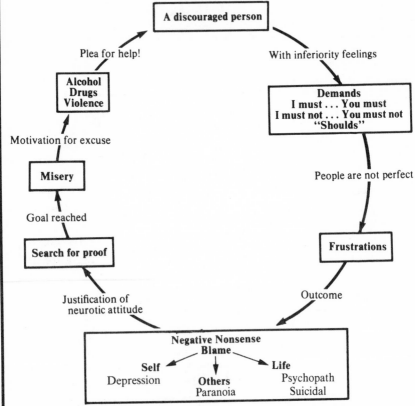

"From O'Connell, Walter: *Essential Readings on Natural High Actualization.* Chicago: North American Graphics, 1981. Order from Alfred Adler Institute, 159 North Dearborn, Chicago, Illinois 60601."

12
Understanding Teenagers

Many parents don't like teenagers, especially their own. There is also a minority group of parents who feel living with teenagers is an exciting, challenging and satisfying experience.

It's possible for any adult to join the fortunate minority. It isn't easy or automatic. But if we can learn to watch and to guide our offspring as they grow from childhood to adulthood, life can be interesting, fulfilling and rejuvenating.

One man who enjoyed children was a poet.

> *Your children are not your children*
> *they are the sons and daughters of life's longing for itself*
> *You may give them your love but not your thoughts*
> *For they have their own thoughts.*
> *You may house their bodies but not their souls,*
> *For their souls dwell in the house of tomorrow*
> *Which you cannot visit, not even in your dreams.*
> *You may strive to be like them*
> *But seek not to make them like you.*
>
> *—Kahlil Gibran "On Children"*

And yet, so many parents fear the mystifying threat of their children becoming teenagers. They are terrified of the impending nightmares of drugs, driving, sex, and alcohol. They hear of friends' youngsters dropping out of school and getting into trouble with the law, and they feel guilty when their children start being violently disobedient and disrespectful to their parents and teachers.

They cringe when adolescents say, "I hate you." "You are old-fashioned and do not understand me." "I want to go away and live my own life." "School is a bore." "My life is wrecked." "The only fun for me is being with my friends or listening to records." "I want to commit suicide."

What is going on? These young people seem to crave independence and instant gratification, and yet are too immature to handle it. What they say doesn't make sense, yet, they aren't the most confused group in society—their parents are!

So often we find a fortyish, tired father confronted with unrealized dreams and hopes about his career, business, sex, success, money and status. He is frantic because he is supposed to raise and guide his son, who is now on the threshold of developing his aspirations for power and accomplishment, and dreaming his own great dreams for the future. If father hasn't done too well in the past twenty years, how is he going to make a success of his son? Even the athletic ability of adolescent muscles is a threat and confirmation to an already discouraged man, now with a new paunch protruding under his belt and his endurance on the tennis court disappearing.

The teenager, by youth alone, has the world by the tail, while the father feels he is losing his grip.

What about mothers? Mothers of adolescents are also at a crisis time in their lives in which their mirrors, emotions and fatigue level tell them discouraging facts about the loss of youth, vim, vigour and sex. To be confronted daily with a vivacious, beautiful and seductive daughter is sometimes overwhelming competition, especially for father's attention and affection.

The emotional mood swings of a menopausal woman unhappily don't jibe with the ecstasies and depressions of adolescence. Often there is a bonding empathy and love between mother and teenager that triggers each to excitement, anger, aggravation or sulking in silent temper tantrums.

Mother love is based on one becoming two, yet still joined somehow. And it is very hard for a mother to accept the real separation that comes from the healthy maturation of her child, when one finally does become two.

For many fathers, mothers, sons and daughters this is the most trying time of their lives, when head-on collisions seem to be the norm rather than the exception.

Competition

What's the cause of all this family conflict and fighting? The reason is competition and lack of trusting communication.

Most of us were reared in a competitive society. Every family member learned the artful antisocial skills of competing, even at an early age. The inevitable result is a lack of open, frank communication skills between the members of the family. Most people call this breakdown the generation gap.

However, there is a bright side. You can have a family without conflict and tears. In democratic families the difficulties mentioned previously can be overcome by the family members' genuine love, consideration and respect for each other.

Communication

The secret is for families to discuss problems openly in social equality. When Dad is feeling down, the whole family encourages him; when Mom is feeling out of sorts the family rally round and fix things for themselves and for her, too. Happy families really listen to each other, pick up body language with empathy, send messages instead of blaming each other and behave with understanding and real concern for each other. They function as a co-operative unit, realizing that the mental health of one is dependent upon the positive stroking that the whole family is willing to give. The whole family conscientiously works at this kind of communication. The teenagers are trusted. The parents have confidence in the ethical training they have invested in their children for the past twelve years and expect the youngsters to make appropriate choices in tempting situations. Usually, the young people live up to the parents' expectations at an unaware level as a self-fulfilling prophecy.

These parents delight to hear how their sons and daughters solve difficult problems with surprising ingenuity. These families have often opened communication lines earlier with techniques like the family council meeting.

In dealing with young people we must practice a genuine give and take philosophy:

1. We must trust them.

2. We must listen to them actively.

3. We talk with them instead of at them.

4. We watch their body language—it will often tell us more about their moods and feelings than their words.

5. We accept their feelings without criticism.

We never condemn a youngster for feeling as he does. Even if it does not make sense to us, the feelings are very real and often painful to him.

For us to judge by remembering how we felt when we were young is not enough—times and values have changed, and so have our memories. To say, "When I was your age" will block communication.

Adults should avoid all phoniness and be real. Teenagers detest anyone or anything that is fake. They hate to feel cheated and will rebel violently, either overtly or covertly. But all teenagers respect reasonable limits and mutually agreed-upon family rules and guidelines.

Teenage problems are influenced by clothes, hair-styles, fads, dating, driving and social acceptance—particularly by the peer group. This peer group pressure is the value-forming agent and is often stronger than common sense or family traditions and religion.

It is almost impossible to fight against it single-handedly. If you are really concerned about the changing values or behaviour of your teenagers it is a good idea to share ideas with the parents of their friends.

Another way may be to "rap" with the gang, discussing such things as parties, study times, use of money, times of arriving home, use of cigarettes, alcohol, marijuana and other drugs. Getting some of these concepts into the open often avoids a situation in which teenagers get their kicks mostly from deceit and the secrecy of forbidden fruits (covert rebellious behaviour).

If the young feel good about their relationships with parents, they don't feel the hostile pressing need to get even or to be rebellious. They respect their family's democratic values and don't seek ways to abuse their parents. Their desire for independence becomes a healthy interdependence.

If you want to help your teenager solve some of his problems, be a model rather than a critic and behave in such a way that you don't appear to add to his problems. Be positive and encouraging. Communicate that you are willing to help and sit down to talk person-to-person over a cup of tea or glass of milk at a quiet time.

Be involved by not thinking about something else—cooking or laundry, reading the paper, etc. Give your undivided attention. Listen actively. Don't push him with probing embarrassing questions; let him share with you what is comfortable for him. A question and answer period is not a respectful conversation.

A direct, intimate question may insult him and increase the barrier that blocks further communication. If he feels a helping relationship of trust, he will be more willing to open up. Don't attempt to solve his problems for him. Show your confidence by allowing him to make his own mistakes and accept the consequences, and he will mature through the process.

The Law

Teenagers who get in trouble with the law come from three specific types of parents. Those who are permissive, and let their kids do their own thing; those who overprotect their children and categorically defend them, claiming that their sons and daughteres are always right, and those who autocratically demand to be obeyed regardless of reason or explanations. These families have never faced reality with problem-solving discussions.

The parents who maintain a healthy balance of caring yet not smothering tend to raise the most responsible teenagers. They are able to love and accept their teenagers as persons, but firmly reject the occasional behaviour that is negative. As Dr. Dreikurs often said, "We should separate the deed from the doer, the act from the actor, and reject the behaviour but not the person." Your teenager does not need you to always agree with him. He is often provocative to test his newly acquired arguments against your mature wisdom. The ages of life between thirteen and fifteen are the most selfish years of life. Later on, more concern for others develops.

In the last century, pioneer children knew their place, helped on the family farm, learned the home-making arts from their mothers or became skilled at their father's trade. Now the choices for the young are wide open. No one really knows their place. Ideals are for others, while they themselves have feelings of insecurity and alienation.

Adolescents, due to their discouragement, may resort to destructive goals as a protest against their fear of non-acceptance. They have not really developed positive social interests. To help them, we must recognize their faulty private logic and guide them into constructive activities through which they will find joy in achievement, satisfaction through helping others and a sense of worth through their own creativity and contribution.

If you, as a parent, teacher or counsellor find this task devastatingly difficult, remember that you are not alone. It isn't impossible for a parent and teenager to give each other joy and happiness. All you need remember is to—

1. give generously of yourself.

2. listen carefully.

3. work at being a supportive, loving and concerned adult.

4. free him from his mistaken goals.

5. give him the courage to be imperfect and release his potential that is held down by fear.

6. redirect him into being a contributing person with feelings of belonging.

These six ideas are the passwords into the happy minority. It doesn't cost money, only time and patience. Join today!

Treat your adolescent as you would treat a friend—with love and respect.

Chart 9

How to recognize and correct teenage misbehaviour

by Pearl Cassel ©

TEENAGER'S BEHAVIOUR (Disturbing to Teachers and Parents)	MISTAKEN GOAL	ADULT'S BASIC REACTION	CONFRONTATION	TECHNIQUE FOR CHANGE
Speed (riding motorcycles, etc.) Valdalism Drugs Alcohol Theft Running Away	Daring Excitement	Fear Guilt Outrage	"Could it be that you did that to prove your courage?" "Could it be that you do this to prove you belong?" "Could it be that you want to impress others?"	"I" messages Open-ended discussions Group work Referral to Agencies
Tardiness—occasional Incomplete assignments Complaining Copying Sloughing off (riding on group project)	Avoidance of work	Threatened Anger Hurt Indignation	"Could it be that you feel that you do not neet to share in the work load?" "Could it be that you think that the work isn't important?"	Group Counselling Class Discussion Use work-contracts between adult and teenager.
Rough play Promiscuity Provocative clothes Obscenity Smoking	Sex	Envious Horrified Arousal Anxiety	"Could it be that you want to be popular with the opposite sex?"	Group dynamics Alternatives
Underground concerts Underground cults Strikes Arguments against norms Petitions Complaints Tardiness-habitual Truancy	Bucking the Establishment	Insecurity Threatened Defensive Exasperated Defeated Hurt Challenged	"Could it be that you want to buck the Establishment?"	Openness Compromise
Quitting job or school Depression Suicide threats	Confrontation with adults	Depressed Hopelessness	"Could it be that you want to break away from your parents?"	Active listening Redefining parent roles Giving support limits Role Playing Life-style analysis
Drug dependencies Addictions: alcohol, tobacco Suicide attempts	Instant gratification Pleasure-seeking	Desperation Disgust Horror I have lost my son/daughter.	"Could it be that looking for pleasure is your main purpose in life?"	Psychotherapy Religious Counselling Construct a meaning for living.

13
Communicating
With Your
Teenager

When we are mentally well, we reach out for others in both verbal and non-verbal ways. Communication is the raw material of which relationships are made. The basis of a successful family is effective communication between its members.

The Generation Gap

We usually refer to it as the breakdown of communication between parent and teenager. In fact, there has *always* been a gap! By nature, any two generations must be different from each other. The young generation has to find its own way—part of the way of doing this is departing from the parents' way. The differences seem to be more intense today. Today's youth are not lazier or more self-centred than their parents. However, today's teenagers are the first to live in a world that is completely unpredictable. Today change occurs very rapidly, and the threat of destruction looms ahead, so the young are a "now" generation. A respect for the past and planning for the future are less relevant to today's youth.

These are the reasons that most teenagers do not set goals or do not work to achieve them.

Today's youth is not opposed to authority, but it is unwilling to submit to arbitrary authority. Youth is too much aware of our shortcomings and is, therefore, sceptical about us and toward authority and authority figures.

Teenagers now feel that their elders are not always more knowledgeable than they are. Youth is just as knowledgeable in many areas of learning and even more informed because of the communications media.

Youngsters demand an active role in society, since this is an age of participation; therefore, external authority is questioned.

Modern youth is generally honest and open: e.g., the sexual revolution. The change is one of attitude rather than in behaviour. Teenagers feel less inhibited by customs and conventions, and feel free to speak about their feelings. Also they are more willing to discuss matters that were once taboo in polite circles. Thus, in their openness they exhibit a basically more healthy attitude. Feelings are out in the open and can be dealt with rationally and constructively.

The rejection of traditional values and the instituting of new values requires an understanding between the generations— and understanding comes from communication. Communication is a meeting of meanings.

Parents often communicate the opposite of what they want to communicate; e.g., a child can sense tenseness between parents, although he may hear no explanation of it. Mother's anxiety, father's frustration about his work, come through as clear signals to children. Children can feel our feelings and can sense when something is bothering us.

Also, a parent may convey his own insecurity when he wants to communicate that he loves his child; i.e., he may give the child too much money or material things if he is not giving much of his time. Children accept gifts as a poor substitute for what they want most—parental love. Remember that the child needs physical and emotional closeness.

Non-verbal communication is often stronger than verbal in families. Teenagers often send out signals in the form of sighs, frowns, smiles, and gestures because they are not able to put into words what they want to say.

Successful communication with teenagers requires that parents learn to listen to non-verbal communications.

Many families usually share some common patterns of communication:

1. Mother is usually the preferred and primary parent in the adolescent's communication.

2. The adolescent female is usually more likely to initiate communication than is the male.

3. Father and son tend to have the least amount of communication; less than mother and son, mother and daughter, father and daughter.

4. Mother and daughter communication is most difficult when it concerns sex behaviour and unacceptable aspects of one's personality.

Family communication can often be improved with some kind of ritual, such as a night when the family plans to be together; for example, the weekly family council in which conflicts, needs, and problems are discussed.

How you give attention and time to communication is not important. That you do it is important. Quality is more important than quantity.

Barriers to Communication

1. Language
  • Words and expressions mean different things to different people, especially the young.
  • Many words are loaded with underlying emotional content. Using them invokes an emotional response and blocks rational communication.
  • Listen to his "culture" and his friends to pick up word meanings.
  • It is not necessary for you to use this language—just understand it.

2. Expectations or images
  • The image we have of another person may get in the way of what he is trying to say, and may result in a slanted and distorted message.
  • Parents frequently fail to hear their teenagers because they see them as rebels.
  • Teenagers fail to hear their parents because they see them as old fogeys, policemen, or preachers.

- Because of our fixed images, we decide prematurely what others are going to say. We then make erroneous assumptions.

3. *Emotional barriers*
   - Anxiety may begin with the parents' concern for the child's well being, but such concern can easily get out of hand.
   - Fears concerning sexual behaviour and the use of the family car are areas in which communication frequently breaks down.
   - It is crucial that parents remain calm, and give rational and appropriate reasons for their concern.
   - Teenagers who fear their parents' reactions may refuse to communicate.
   - Parents must work at communicating their acceptance of their teenager without necessarily communicating approval of his behaviour.
   - Good behaviour should be given approval.
   - Parents want to be accepted by their teenagers, and may become defensive. The parent who fears rejection may become weak and passive, and do nothing to confront his child. If the parent becomes preoccupied with justifying himself, he will not be able to listen to his child. The result is that of two people talking but not communicating.

4. *Projection of blame on others*
   - The issue is not "Who is to blame?" but rather, "How can we understand each other?"
   - Parents sometimes resort to authoritarianism in an effort to defend themselves when a teenager questions their decisions.
   - The adolescent needs an adequate and appropriate reason.

5. *Examine our expectations for our teenagers*
   - Delicate balance is called for.
   - Know when to take a stand and when to compromise.
   - Beware of becoming involved in trivial issues. Determine priorities—the style of dress and length of hair are not crucial when compared with sexual attitudes, schoolwork and human relations.

It may help you to share your concern with others; e.g., the minister, teachers or others who work with young people at group meetings.

Establishing and Maintaining Dialogue with Your Teenager

1. Work at it!

2. Learn teenager language, but don't talk it. The teenager wants to be understood by you, not copied.

3. Become sensitive to the feelings behind the words.

4. Parents must become good conversationalists and be able to talk about a number of topics. If the only conversations that take place involve problems and crises, they will not be effective. Talk about subjects that are of interest to your teenager—let him know that you are interested in topics that are important to him.

5. The job of communication is more a matter of listening than of speaking.

6. Trivial beginnings often lead to more important matters.

7. Be honest—be yourself—don't hedge—don't be afraid to say, "I don't know." Also, don't be afraid to say, "I believe that..."

8. Generate trust—trust your teenager and be trustworthy yourself. Suspicion and dishonesty are the two great enemies of clear and effective communication.

9. Be consistent—don't give permission to go somewhere, and then create anxiety about his going—give clear permission or clear refusal.

10. Be natural—don't preach, don't use cliches, don't give trite advice.

11. Avoid "When I was your age..." Communicate from who you are now, not who you were "way back when."

12. Speak in simple language—avoid their jargon.

13. Speak with love—avoid being judgmental or over-critical; being over-passive or permissive also produces unfortunate results.

14. To love another person is to take him seriously. Try to be understanding but not patronizing. Teenagers think their conflicts are unique and serious, and are insulted when you try to reassure them with "everyone goes through this."

15. Give of yourself!—Listen carefully!

16. Work at being a loving parent!

For more detailed helpful information regarding communicating with teenagers read *The Challenge of Adolescence,* Guidance Centre, Faculty of Education, University of Toronto, 1985.

14
Awareness Especially for Counsellors

I believe that our strongest link between awareness and knowledge is *sensitivity*. We, as counsellors, are presented with many difficult problems and have been taught to solve them by using our sensitivity and awareness. However, these skills alone are not enough. We need special knowledge as well. Certainly, we must use our sensitivity toward others to become aware of the purpose in their behaviour, but we also need knowledge to guide them. As we all know, in training young children, knowledge of correctional techniques is essential.

It is my hope that we will learn to use our sensitivity and our awareness in five different ways that will help us gain new knowledge to use in our work. The first important awareness is awareness of *ourselves*; the second, awareness of *others* as individuals; the third, awareness of *groups* and their *group* norms; the fourth, awareness of *how* others see and hear us; and the fifth, how to *see* and *hear* others.

This last category, how to *see* and *hear* others, is our most useful counselling tool. It involves learning what makes people do what they do.

People act as individuals or within the group that they belong to, according to their life-styles. We cannot begin to understand a person if we are *prejudiced* against individuals. We can't begin to understand life-style if we only *generalize* about groups. We can't co-operate in our society if we have personal feelings of *superiority* or *inferiority*.

In the year 1900, Alfred Adler discovered that many of his psychiatric patients had developed neurotic symptoms due to their feelings of inferiority and their striving for superiority over others. He realized they had been raised and educated in a competitive setting and he described some of these neurotic symptoms as an expression of the Will to Power. Adler also studied healthy people. He found that when individuals were raised in a co-operative family and educated in a school where children were taught how to feel useful, they developed healthy life-styles and could cope with life's problems as they arose.

It is a sad fact of our society that some people—especially students—tend to measure themselves *against* others. There is a popular song that begins:

> *Everybody's got to have somebody to look down on*
> *We've got to feel superior to those that we frown on*

I suggest this philosophy is a result of competitive—not co-operative—living, where people want the three big P's.

Power, Profit and Prestige

One of the main struggles throughout childhood is to overcome *real* feelings of inferiority—about size, experience, and skills. As each new skill is mastered, at home and at school, the child develops confidence in his abilities and forms a healthy life-style, especially if his parents and teachers are encouraging.

But if children are raised in a competitive family, and trained in a competitive primary classroom, they will learn to look up or down at each other—which causes a psychological pain in the neck. This pain hinders learning and the children become discouraged, and discouragement becomes misbehaviour.

Children devote their energies to striving to become better than others, or to maintain their position of being the best; or they give up trying. These are the results of competitive methods: the stress on the hierarchy of marks; by drill games where there are always winners and losers; by extra rewards given to the children with perfect work.

Sometimes, due to a child's faulty logic, he chooses destructive behaviour in order to feel significant. This often happens with a child under seven years of age because he is forming his life-style and depends on adult reaction, negative or positive, for proof of his status. Older students depend on the peer group for status. They can handle competitive situations without feeling personally put down when they lose.

Alfred Adler stressed that to feel human involves possessing human dignity, and that every human being is deserving of respect for his humanity alone. Mutual respect is the key to open communication and harmonious interpersonal relationships.

Victor Frankl, an active Adlerian psychiatrist, makes this point very clear in his book *Man's Search for Meaning.* As a prisoner in concentration camps during World War II, he found that among his fellow prisoners, those who lost their feelings of personal worth and human dignity gave up and died. Those who found and held on to at least a small fragment of self-respect, despite all the atrocities around them, kept the will to survive.

Adlerians believe that we must respect children in order that they develop self-respect. In teaching or guiding a child we build on strengths, not weaknesses. It's so easy to find out what is wrong with a person, and to point out his deficiencies; but we are much more effective if we concentrate on what a person does right. The power of positive thinking is encouraging to ourselves and to the others that we deal with.

Throughout life it is normal to strive to overcome our own feelings of inferiority. We work to increase our knowledge, skills, and abilities in order to feel better about ourselves and to be more useful to others.

Some individuals who start life with a physical handicap overcompensate in their desire to overcome their deficiency. For example, they may be born with a physical handicap and decide to master specialized skills in order to feel useful, rather than be dependent on others. We can think of artists who have no arms but paint beautiful pictures by holding the brush in their teeth, people, such as Lester Pearson, who be-

gan life with a speech impediment and became excellent public speakers. You may be wondering what makes some people
give up and others struggle on.

Adler answered that man is self-determining and creative.
He *decides* what he will do in any situation. These decisions
form the fabric of his personality. By *positive decision-making*,
we can turn a very difficult problem into an opportunity to
learn for ourselves and then to help others. Man is not merely a
victim of his hereditary endowment.

His ability to cope with problems is an expression of his
mental health. Good mental health depends on his level of
social interest, and by measuring a person's social interest, we
can predict his adjustments. The mentally healthy individual
is *concerned* about others and uses his ability to *co-operate* and
contribute in a social setting.

But how can we help others if we are not sensitive to their
needs, goals, and private motivational logic? *We must attempt
to hear with their ears, see with their eyes, and stand in their shoes.*
Unless we can be aware of what makes a person do what he
does and know what *is* his private logic, we are in no position
to help him.

So, we must use our sensitivity to become aware of a student's immdiate goals, and his long-range life goals, then use
our guidance techniques to help him make better choices regarding his social behaviour, his academic learning, or his
course selection.

The Dangers of Sensitivity

Just being sensitive is not enough. We must use our sensitivity only as a guide to what to do next. When teaching or counselling young children, sensitivity can be a handicap. As we
discussed in Chapter 6, expressing our emotions openly is the
worst possible technique for training the misbehaving child,
since it *reinforces* the child's misbehaviour.

The mentally healthy child has good feelings about himself
and his goals are *constructive*. The two main constructive goals
are (1) to learn, and (2) to be co-operative. The four mistaken goals are destructive to social order.

If adults respond to their gut feelings when dealing with the
misbehaving child, they further reinforce the child's faulty

logic and convince the child that this behaviour has satisfied his mistaken goal.

If the student makes us be angry and shout in order to force him to learn, we are not teaching or training but inviting rebellion. Shouting at children to make them obey is like steering your car with the horn.

Students have two pet hates about teachers. Young children hate yellers, and older students can't stand boring teachers.

It is important to be aware of our feelings, when training children; but we should not react with our negative emotions. Instead we *confront* the child with the purpose of his misbehaviour or intentions in his mistaken goals, and watch for his recognition reflex.

This confrontation involves our specific counselling skills of establishing rapport, being aware of body language, enlisting co-operation, actively listening to the child and influencing him to listen to us.

Changing Goals

Having recognized our own emotional reaction, controlled it, and hidden it, we can actively set about helping the child to change his goal from negative to positive purposes, by using specialized techniques that are classified as corrective procedures.

We can be more effective if we also instruct the child's teacher and his parents in these special training techniques. For example, if we have confronted the child about the purpose of his behaviour, and he has shown a "recognition reflex" to the question Could it be that you want the teacher's attention? we can then advise the teacher to give the child attention at the times when the child does not demand it. We can also suggest to the parents that their child seems to feel significant only when doing negative things to demand mother's attention. A mother can also learn to take notice of the child only when he is displaying co-operative behaviour. This technique is likely to produce improvement and a happier child.

Nobody does anything without a goal or purpose as his motivation. Not you, not a student, not even a two-week-old baby.

If you want to understand a student's behaviour, don't look for causes—find the consequences. Think—what was the payoff for him?

We must remember that the student's goal may be at an unaware level. Also, we must remember that healthy people get a sense of pleasure from contributing. They feel good when they know that they have gained skills and accomplishments, or have been helpful to others. On the other hand, poorly adjusted people have unhealthy goals and seek negative payoffs. Their payoff may be getting someone angry, upset or miserable. We must realize that some students come to school for only one purpose—to make the teacher's *life as miserable as possible*.

By discussing causes, we only give a student an extra excuse for misbehaving. A student may feel entitled to do his own thing, and not respect the needs of others. He may feel that the school is unfair to him because he is being taught by a boring teacher.

So what! Many students cope in spite of these difficulties. With our support, and directive counselling, he can learn to cope with those problems, too; the problem of smoking is an example. I suggest that we look at the intentions of the student's behaviour. The consequence of his smoking may be that his parents get angry, and his intention may be to do the opposite of his parents' wishes; or to buck the establishment; or to feel that he is big and powerful.

The technique of confronting a student with a question regarding his intentions not only increases his own awareness of his behaviour, but "spits in his psychologial soup," which in the future may not be as palatable any more. Then the student is free to choose for himself, and once he changes his *goals* he can then change his *behaviour*. He needs our help to start the change process.

Behaviour Modification

At this point, I would like to comment on behaviour modification. The behaviour modifier only deals with behaviour, not motivations or goals. For a student to transfer from extrinsic to intrinsic motivation may be a slow process or impossible. Adlerians believe that between the "stimulus" and the "response" is a creative, self-determining human being who decides and makes choices about whether he is willing to be conditioned or not. From this viewpoint the ideal intervention program is designed by consultation with the student so that it becomes self-modification.

Adlerians think about *modification* of the *motivation* of behaviour, not just the behaviour itself, i.e. Motivation Modification rather than Behaviour Modification.

For those of us who deal with students aged ten or over, the counselling techniques are very different from those used in training primary grade children.

The Six Teenage Goals

The private logic of teenagers who are troubled, perhaps involves one of the four mistaken goals of young children, but more likely involves one of the six adolescent goals of discouraged behaviour (see Chart 9).

The six teenage goals are as follows:

1. Daring and excitement

2. Avoidance of work

3. Sex

4. Bucking the establishment

5. Contradiction of adult opinion

6. Instant gratification (search for pleasure).

The sixth mistaken goal, their quest for instant gratification, explains their hedonistic attitude. Hence, their experimentation with alcohol and the drug scene.

These six goals are usually negative, and an overt expression of discouraged kids. Youngsters who desperately want to belong to a group are willing to sell out values that they have learned in the family, church or school. It has been proven that discouragement about finding one's place produces misbehaviour.

Peer group pressure becomes the value-forming agent in adolescence, and the fear of group rejection becomes the motivating force. Counselling teenagers in groups, therefore, is very effective, but the counsellor must be skilled enough to confront the group with their negative values and to guide the students into more constructive behaviour. Heightened awareness of self and others is the most vital experience in the group dynamic.

There is also a place for private counselling of the troubled teenager. The counsellor begins with a life-style analysis. He asks the student specific questions about his family structure, his parents, his siblings; how he sees his position in the family constellation; how he feels about being the eldest child, the middle, or the youngest; or, how he feels about being the only boy in the family, how he perceives his role as the only child. If his family is competitive, whom did he compete against—his father, brother or even a sister? How did he compete as a child? What are his early recollections, dreams, and actual goals in life?

Collecting this information takes about an hour and can also be done in groups. It is a fascinating experience for us as well as the student. Once this data is collected, we can then attempt to interpret his life-style.

Is he a Controller, a Getter, or a Pleaser? (See Chapter 4.) All life-styles are established in early childhood and can only be changed from one typology to another by therapy. However, we must remember that there is no such thing as a good or bad life-style. Each person uses his own life-style for negative or positive purposes. As counsellors, we can help a student to redirect his behaviour within his own life-style towards constructive rather than destructive actions. It is at this point that we use not just our sensitivity but our knowledge so that we can help the student to make better choices.

If we know that a student is troubled or discouraged, we must make special efforts to encourage him whenever possible. We should make a point of seeing and talking to him frequently, even if only with a brief greeting in our office, in the halls, and in his classroom. We must let him know that we care. We must convince him that he is important to us, because most discouraged students firmly believe that nobody cares about them, and they feel worthless.

In order to help you to further understand the idea of purposive behaviour, I would like to discuss the five basic premises of Adlerian psychology (see Chapter 7).

We as counsellors, are preparing our students to face the main tasks of life.

Using the Five Premises

The first premise is that all of our behaviour is socially embedded, and that all of our problems are social problems. The three most important life-problem areas—occupation, sex, and society—are all basically social in nature. We all need a sense of belonging, and any time that need is frustrated, we feel alienated, and so function with reduced skill and poor mental or physical health.

Tension, our personal enemy, grows out of our resistance to and resentment about the requirements of life.

Instead of leaving this problem to be treated by doctors or psychiatrists, many wise teachers and counsellors in senior schools are actively teaching students the invaluable art of relaxation by transcendental meditation, physical techniques, etc.

Adler understood that a child's self-confidence and his personal courage are his greatest good fortune. The child must be educated to share, and also to contribute to the community. Therefore, his teachers must have well-developed social interests themselves. Good teachers are confident and aware of their own place in life and are not dependent on students for their status. They never do for a child what he can do for himself. A child who finds an adult who is willing to be his servant is deprived of his feeling of growth and independence, and is actually insulted. In order to foster healthy growth we must give responsibility.

Adlerians firmly believe that *all behaviour is socially embedded*, and that we constantly strive to find our place in a group. In our early years, this group is our family; later, the school; then the peer group and finally, the community. The social group is our focus and all of our behaviour is movement toward the group, within the group, or away from the group.

We make strenuous efforts in our behaviour for acceptance, approval, and recognition. People who accept us—recognize our efforts and show their approval—are encouraging. We feel encouraged by these positive strokes, or "warm fuzzies." Everyone likes "warm fuzzies" and is hurt by "cold pricklies."

A discouraged person loses confidence, self-esteem and the will or ability to contribute. His feelings of self-worth decrease, and his behaviour may become destructive to himself and others.

Such discouraged individuals may become tyrants or criminals. Others escape from their loneliness into drug abuse or alcoholism, since they feel left out or useless.

The well-adjusted person who feels a sense of belonging and well-being about himself behaves in accordance with his situation. The student who cannot cope needs you. Perhaps he feels that the situation has trapped him and he can't see his way out without very specific help and guidance. If he is physically, emotionally and mentally healthy, your help will be only temporary—a good dose of encouragement.

On the other hand, if he is maladjusted he will have faulty concepts about himself and others. His feelings of inferiority or superiority may be over-emphasized. He will need ongoing counselling or psychiatric help.

One may ask, "What is the difference between a psychiatrist, a counsellor, and a teacher?" Dr. Dreikurs, Adler's most famous student, told us that the only difference is academic qualification and the time available to counsel the discouraged person. All three are educators, and therapy is an educational process.

Dr. Murray Banks has explained the difference between a neurotic and psychotic. The neurotic builds dream castles in the air; the psychotic moves in, and the psychiatrist collects the rent. Good therapy, good counselling and good teaching involve respecting the individual, increasing his awareness, and influencing him to change from ignorance to knowledge. All these processes help a person to change from faulty concepts and confused thinking to constructive decision-making.

You may be wondering how to tell the difference between the student who just needs a temporary crutch and the one who needs more lengthy treatment. The answer is within his life-style.

The second basic assumption of individual psychology is that we are self-determining and creative. We are active participants who not only react but *act*. We are *not* victims of our drives. We decide what we will do, and therefore we *can* change. Our students can change if they want to. We must use our counselling skills to motivate them.

Adler's third basic assumption is that all behaviour is purposive, or, as they say in the jargon—teleological. Behaviour is goal-directed towards finding one's place in society.

Adler's fourth premise is that we are subjective in our perceptions which means that for each of us, reality is dependent on our perception of it. And our perception is likely to be biased or mistaken.

The fifth Adlerian principle is that we observe the person from a holistic viewpoint. This means that the whole is more than the sum total of its parts—the synergistic effect. To understand a person, we look at repeated patterns of behaviour and not at isolated incidents.

Within these five Adlerian premises, I would like to again consider awareness.

Awareness of Self

Let us become more aware of our own strengths. Counselling is a vital job in society. We have the skills to help children, to help teachers, and to help the community. Let us not be put down by people who are ignorant of the importance of our work. When necessary, we must find the courage, time, and energy to promote our profession. We know that every junior school needs a full time counselor, so why not use our skills to influence boards of education and bring about that much needed change? Counselling of juniors is preventive–to avoid more tragic and expensive problems later.

We continue to spend so much time in crisis intervention, and are denied the opportunity to work with healthy young children where we could be most useful to society. We could set up programs to actually help children develop decision-making skills, and work with teachers and parents in developmental guidance. An ounce of prevention is still worth a pound of cure—despite the metric system!

Awareness of Others as Individuals

When counselling students we have to be aware of their goals and motivations, whether they are negative or positive; only then can we draw from our variety of techniques to give each and every student the feeling that we personally care about him.

If we can accept the fact that we are self-determining and creative; if we believe that our own behaviour is purposive and goal-directed even at an unaware level; then we may find it easier to be able to answer for ourselves some soul-searching questions about our jobs as counsellors:

- Who am I?
- What am I doing?
- Where am I going?
- What is my life-style?
- Am I a Pleaser, a Controller, a Driver, etc.?
- Do I need to be liked, to be good, to be right, or to be superior to others?

Once we come up with some relatively realistic answers for ourselves, we are in a better position to be consciously aware of others as individuals and to respect them for their individuality. Try to take a short course on life-style, or meet regularly with a group of friends to diagnose each other.

Awareness of Groups with Their Group Norms

Do we know what values to accept and what to reject? We have just learned to always accept *the person*; we must also be aware of when and how to reject their *behaviours*, and do something actively to bring about change. We should separate the deeds from the doers, the acts from the actors.

Do we really know how children act away from school? Do we find out by reading their magazines or asking what they watch on TV? Do we wander through a store to become aware of their fashion fads; or sometimes go to the places where they go—the rock concerts, the track, the football game, the swimming pool, their local shopping plaza, and their dances? By briefly involving ourselves in their sub-culture we can understand more about them.

At times, our students may be involved in illegal behaviour such as smoking pot or drinking alcoholic beverages. We must be strong enough to confront them, discuss the possible consequences of their actions with them, and use our influence to guide them toward more constructive activities.

Awareness of How Others See and Hear Us

Do we have the courage to find out how people perceive us? What do they see and hear? We can check our appearance in a mirror and tape our voices, but do we also have the courage to ask how we are coming across? Do we create an impression of trust, encouraging a student to share his thoughts and feelings with us? Are we warm and friendly or cold and distant? Are we aware of our body language? If we find out aspects of ourselves that need improvement, are we willing to change? Students learn more from a model than from a critic.

How to See and Hear Others

We can sharpen our awareness of others if we try to see with their eyes, hear with their ears, and stand in their shoes. We will then have greater insights and more ideas about how to be of help. Ideas, however, are curious things—they won't work unless we do.

There *are* ways to overcome the most difficult situations if we have faith in ourselves. Our sensitivity, our awareness, and our knowledge are the strengths we have. We have but to use them.

To be an effective teacher we must be aware of and sensitive to the needs of others; the Ministry, our board of education, our area superintendents, our principals, the staff, parents and particularly our students. Teaching is an exercise in human relationships and communication skills. Unless we have a healthy relationship and good rapport with a pupil we cannot teach him anything.

We must be aware of others as individuals;

aware of groups with their group norms;

aware of how others see and hear us;

aware of how to see and hear others.

Mostly we must be aware of ourselves, and that means clarifying our own values.

An emotionally healthy person can cope, and make appropriate adjustments to life situations.

An emotionally healthy person is aware of his feelings, attitudes, values and beliefs. He is in touch with himself. He can talk clearly with his inner self and also communicate effectively with others. He is fully functioning, self-activated or integrated; and is developing social interest.

There are eight criteria for emotional maturity. In order of importance, they are as follows:

1. To love and feel loved

2. To be creative

3. To have the ability to deal constructively with reality

4. To have the capacity to change—be flexible

5. To be free from tension symptoms, e.g., headaches, ulcers, dependence on crutches. (Tension grows out of resentment and resistance to life's problems.)

6. To be more satisfied with giving than receiving

7. To have the ability to relate to others in a consistent way

8. To have the ability to sublimate one's own hostile energy into creative constructive outlets.

Appendix

1. How to Analyse Your Own Life-Style

Character traits rating form

Part one

1 As a child under five years whose approval did you seek most?
   Father _____ Mother _____ Both _____
   Neither _____

2 Whose approval did you get most?
   Father _____ Mother _____ Both _____
   Neither _____

3 Can you accept criticism without being hurt?
   Yes _____ No _____

If answers to 1 and 2 match you are probably confident and able to handle criticism without getting upset. If they do not match you are probably vulnerable to criticism.

Part two

Rate yourself in the traits listed below as you remember you were before age eight.
   A Above average   **B** Average   **C** Below average

Also rate yourself in comparison to any of your siblings.
1 Most **2** Average **3** Least

	Personal grade (A, B, or C)	Relationship to siblings (1, 2, or 3)
Intelligence		
Grades		
Industrious		
Standards of achievement		
Athletic		
Daring		
Good looks		
Feminine		
Masculine		
Obedient		
Made mischief		
Openly rebellious		
Covertly rebellious		
Punished		
Standards of right-wrong		
Critical of others		
Methodical/neat		
Withdrawn		
Critical of self		
Easy going		
Charming		
Pleasing		
Cheerful		
Sociable		
Sense of humor		
Considerate		
Bossy		
Demanded own way		
Temper		
Fighter		
Chip on shoulder		
Sulked		
Stubborn		
Shy		
Sensitive and easily hurt		

	Personal grade (A, B, or C)	*Relationship to siblings (1, 2, or 3)*
Idealistic	————	————
Materialistic	————	————
Responsible	————	————
Excitement-seeker	————	————

Now mark the character traits that you rated yourself A or 1. Match your list with the lists in the life-style themes in Chart 1 (page 136). This will give you an indication of your life-style. Now refer back to typologies starting on page 23.

Example–Joan rated herself A or 1 in the following character traits: Selfishness   Materialistic
Having own way   and rebellious
Temper tantrums

She is probably a Getter and could refer to page 23.

Chart 1

Suggested templates for sibling ratings & general life-style themes

Life-style Theme	Rated themselves *Most* when compared to other siblings		
Getter	Selfishness Having own way	Temper tantrums Materialistic	Rebellious Sensitives
Driver	Hardest worker Critical of others	Best grades Idealistic	Standards of accomplishment
Controller	Critical of others Rebellious	Intelligent (Least) Spontaneous	Having own way Standards of accomplishment
Need to be right	Critical of others	Trying to please Best grades	Sensitive easily hurt
Need to be superior	Selfishness Temper tantrums Idealistic	Strongest Attractive	Most athletic Having own way
Need to be liked	Trying to please Considerate	Punished Conforming Attractive	Help around house Sensitive easily hurt
Need to be good	Conforming Hardest worker	Most athletic Idealistic	Critical of others Standards of accomplishment
Aginner	Rebellious Spoiled	Temper tantrums	Sensitive- easily hurt
Victim	Idealistic	Punished	Sensitive- easily hurt
Martyr	Trying to please	Sensitive- easily hurt	Idealistic Punished
Baby	Having own way Attractive	Selfishness Spoiled	Temper tantrums

Inadequate person	Trying to please
	(Low) intelligence
		Sensitive-
		  easily hurt
			(Low) standards of
			  accomplishment . . .

Avoids feelings	Intelligent	Standards of accomplishment	Best grades Comforming
Excitement seeker	Sense of humor Rebellious	Spoiled Selfishness	Spontaneous Idealistic

Eckstein, Daniel and Baruth, 1975

Chart 2

Decision-making

A recent study of adolescent students suggested that there are a variety of personal decision-making strategies commonly used.

Compliant
This person prefers to let someone else decide for him/her. "Whatever you say, sir."

Delaying
This person can't make up his/her mind to decide. "I'll do it later. What's the big rush?"

Fatalistic
This person thinks that what will be will be, so why decide. "It's all in the cards."

Planning
This person is an organized decision-maker who carefully weighs alternatives before deciding. He/she follows a definite strategy.

Impulsive
This person decides and afterwards thinks about the decision.

Agonizing
This person searches for so much information that the decision get so complex, he/she is "lost in the confusion."

Intuitive
This person uses more feeling than thinking. "It feels right inside so I think I'll do it." This is a mystical choice.

Adolescents benefit from being taught the following logical decision-making process:

Paralysis
This person knows he/she must decide but is so overwhelmed by the choices that he/she is unable to make any decision at all.

Logical Decision-making

1. Define the problem.
2. List the alternatives.
3. Identify the criteria, including personal values.
4. Evaluate the alternatives with the criteria.
5. Determine the best alternative but consider consequences.
6. Make the decision.

2. Dreikurisms

A child needs encouragement as a plant needs water.

●

You should never feel sorry for a child. To do so gives him justification to feel sorry for himself; and no one is as unhappy as someone who feels sorry for himself.

●

If we can learn to keep our mouths shut, we can learn anything.

●

So often, what we do to correct a child is responsible for his not improving.

●

Nothing is as pathetic as a defeated authority who does not know he is defeated.

●

We spend more time with an untrained child than we do in training the child.

●

We should give the child attention—but not at the times he demands it.

●

Unfortunately, those who need encouragement the most get it the least, because they behave in such a way that our reaction to them pushes them further into discouragement and rebellion.

●

When you spank the child it is because you don't know anything better to do.

●

We must realize we do not teach children how to take on responsibility as long as we take on the responsibility for them.

●

If training were as simple as setting a good example, we would not find so many irresponsible children coming from homes where the parents are so resonsible.

●

It's not the quantity of time spent with our children that is important, but the quality.